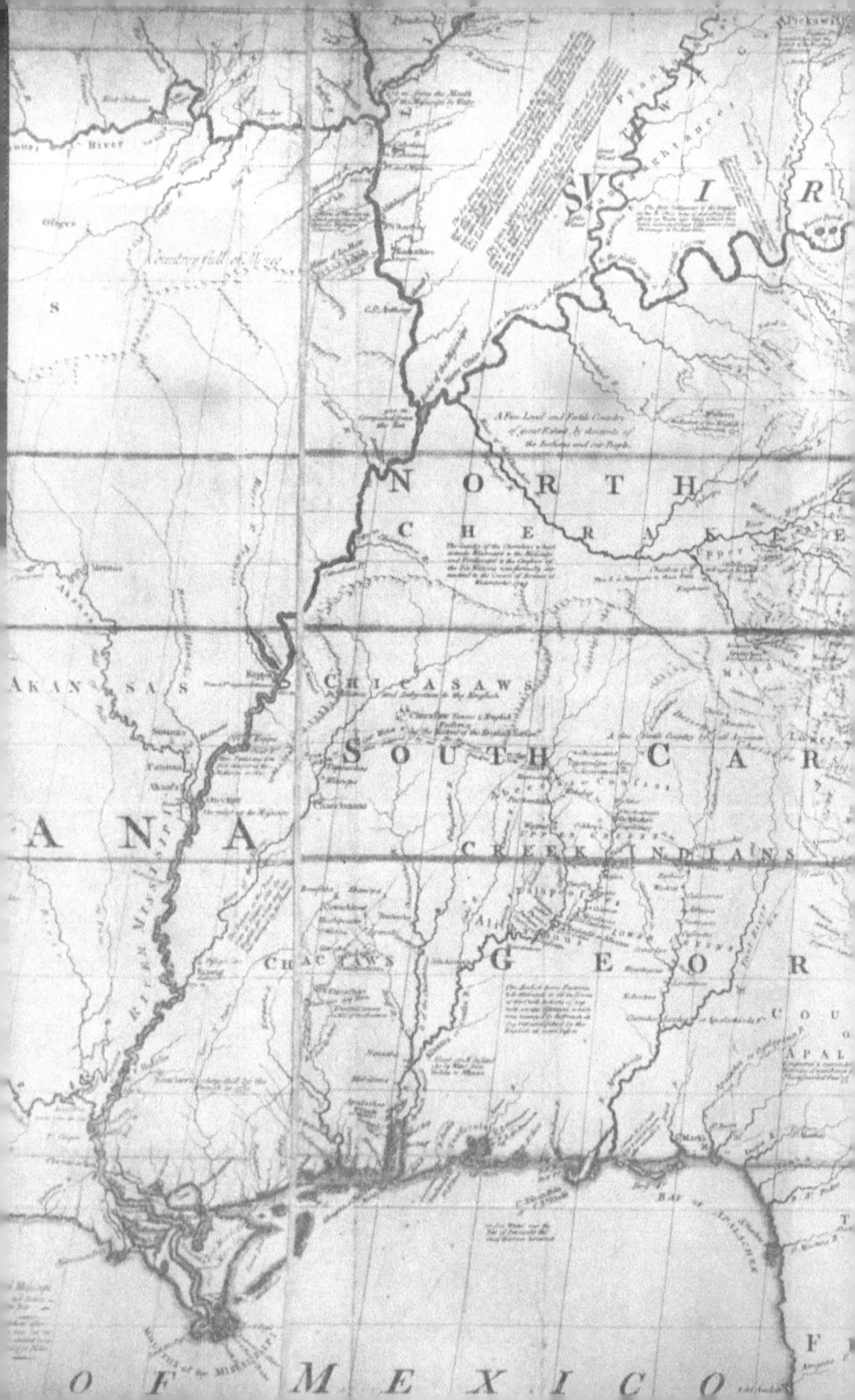

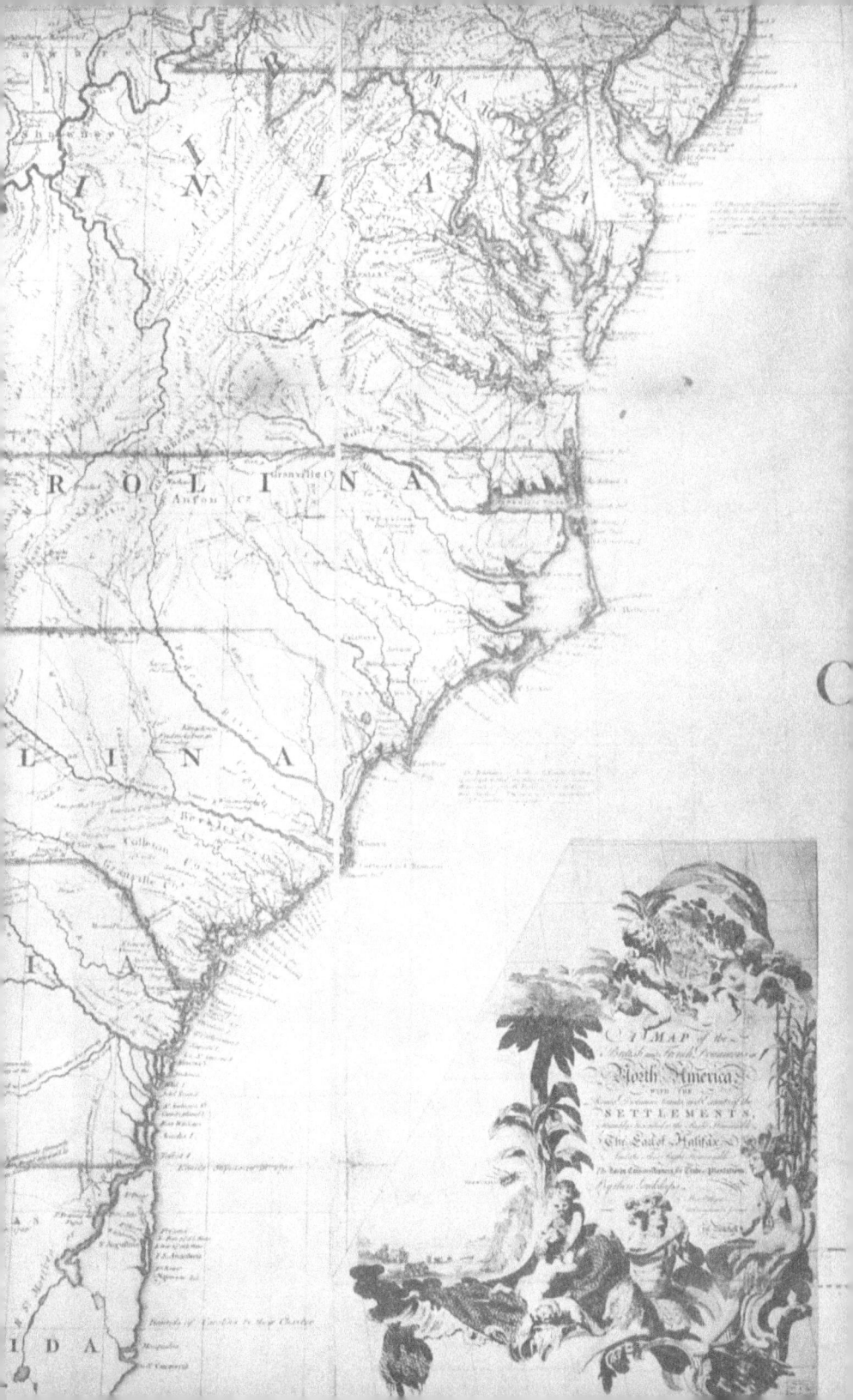

TRADE AND TRAVEL AROUND THE
SOUTHERN APPALACHIANS

American Stage Wagon. From *Travels through the States of North America and the Provinces of Upper and Lower Canada, during the Years 1795, 1796 and 1797*, by Isaac Weld.

Trade and Travel Around The Southern Appalachians Before 1830

By

RANDLE BOND TRUETT

Chapel Hill
The University of North Carolina Press
1935

COPYRIGHT, 1935, BY
THE UNIVERSITY OF NORTH CAROLINA PRESS

PRINTED AND BOUND IN THE UNITED STATES OF AMERICA
BY THE SEEMAN PRINTERY, INC., DURHAM, NORTH CAROLINA
THIS BOOK WAS DIGITALLY PRINTED.

To

MY MOTHER AND FATHER
Annie Bond Truett
Harry Love Truett

PREFACE

A MASS of literature has been published during the last decade pertaining to western migration. The impetus that started this great avalanche of historical writing was Dr. Frederick Jackson Turner's thought provoking study, "The Significance of the Frontier." Many phases have claimed the attention of writers, but the topic that I am considering seems to have been neglected. Few writers interested themselves in the section known as the Old Southwest, and in particular the route south of the mountains into this area.

The field of this study consists of Georgia, Alabama, Mississippi, and Louisiana; in other words, those states situated south of the southern terminus of the mountains. The time limit has been arbitrarily set to coincide with the introduction of the railroad, 1830, when conditions were materially changed, and a new and distinct period was introduced.

Peter J. Hamilton, in his *Colonial Mobile,* stated that, "No more important study can be found than that of the early roads, for along them poured immigration which has claimed the Southwest for the Anglo-Saxon civilization."

The importance and value of the history of early travel has recently been stated by V. Heber Sergeant, in an article "The First Road of All":

Anyone who wants to study seriously the earliest history of America, cannot get a better foundation for doing so than to make a study of the early wilderness trails, for it was along them and upon them that all the events of history took place—and it is along modern highways constructed, in many instances, over the exact routes of these early wilderness trails that we drive our cars . . . when we go "a touring." *The Highway Magazine,* Vol. XXIII (1932), No. 3, p. 65.

It has been my good fortune to travel through practically all of the territory considered. It was indeed a sensation to travel over in one hour sixty miles of the same road, through the same forests, over the same creeks and rivers, that one hundred years ago required three whole days to cover.

A word of explanation is necessary concerning Chapter VI and Appendix II, which deal with inns and taverns. The list (Appendix II) is far more complete than any published thus far, but it still has many wide gaps that need to be filled before it can approach any degree of completeness. It would require more time and a great amount of travel to complete the section and when completed it would be a study in itself rather than merely one chapter in a book.

I wish to thank Dr. William C. Binkley, Dr. Frank L. Owsley, and Dr. Carl S. Driver of Vanderbilt University, and Dr. George M. McBride of the University of California at Los Angeles for their council and assistance. The Bureau of Public Roads of the Department of Agriculture in Washington, D. C., made available to me their collections of pictures and literature concerning early travel. I wish to thank the librarians in the following libraries for their coöperation: Alabama State Archives, Montgomery, Ala.; Bureau of Public Roads, Department of Agriculture, Washington, D. C.; Carnegie Library, Nashville, Tenn.; Filson Club Library, Louisville, Ky.; George Peabody Library, Nashville, Tenn.; Huntington Library, San Marino, Calif.; Kentucky Historical Society Library, Frankfort, Ky.; Library of Congress, Washington, D. C.; Los Angeles Public Library; Louisiana State Historical Society Library, New Orleans; Louisville Free Public Library; Calvin M. McClung Historical Collection, Lawson McGhee Library, Knoxville, Tennessee; Mississippi Historical Society Library, Jackson, Miss.; New Orleans Public Library; Pasadena Public Library; Public Library, Columbus, Ga.; Tennessee State Historical Society Library, Nashville, Tenn.; Tennessee State Library, Nashville, Tenn.; Transylvania College Library, Lexington, Ky.; University of California at Los Angeles Library; University of Louisville Library; University of Southern California Library, Los Angeles, Calif.; Vanderbilt University Library, Nashville, Tenn. I would like to express my appreciation to Dr. J. Franklin Bradley of the Department of English at the University of Louisville, for his help in reading the manuscript. I also want to express my indebtedness to my wife, Elizabeth Miller Truett, for her untiring efforts in reading and correcting the manuscript and for typing the final copy.

RANDLE BOND TRUETT.

Lincoln Ridge, Kentucky
August 5, 1933

CONTENTS

	PAGE
PREFACE	vii

CHAPTER
- I. INDIAN TRAILS OR TRACES ... 3
- II. TRADING PATHS OF THE EARLY SETTLERS ... 16
- III. IMMIGRATION SOUTH OF THE MOUNTAINS ... 37
- IV. THE DEVELOPMENT OF POST ROADS ... 50
- V. THE TRAVELER ON THE ROAD ... 79
- VI. INNS AND TAVERNS OF THE OLD SOUTH ... 98
- VII. IMPROVEMENTS IN TRANSPORTATION ... 116
- VIII. MODES OF CONVEYANCE ... 131
    - APPENDIX I. EXPORTS FROM SOUTHERN PORTS, 1790-1820 ... 139
    - APPENDIX II. INNS AND TAVERNS. AN ANNOTATED LIST, GEOGRAPHICALLY AND CHRONOLOGICALLY ARRANGED ... 142
    - BIBLIOGRAPHY ... 160
    - INDEX ... 183

ILLUSTRATIONS

AMERICAN STAGE WAGON..........................*Frontispiece*

Facing page
THE RELAY 68

MAP SHOWING PROPOSED ROUTES BETWEEN
    WASHINGTON AND NEW ORLEANS........................ 76

OLD STAGE COACH... 100

RAIL-ROAD ACCIDENT...................................... 128

A SOUTHERN WAGON SHOWING CONESTOGA INFLUENCE........ 132

TRADE AND TRAVEL AROUND THE SOUTHERN APPALACHIANS

CHAPTER I
INDIAN TRAILS OR TRACES

IN THE old Southwest one finds the termination of the Alleghany Mountains, extending through northern Georgia and Alabama. It was around the southern end of these mountains that the early trader and traveler found his way, a way that was not obstructed as were the paths of the western movement farther north.

Ellen Churchill Semple said that "The westward expansion of the American people has been marked by a slow advance from tidewater to 'fall line,' and from 'fall line' across the Alleghenies."[1] This is not altogether true in the South. They did move from the tidewater to the fall line, but in the South they continued along the fall line into the western country. The geological line played an important part in western movement in the South.

The coastal plain extends inland until it meets the harder structure that forms the piedmont, and the juncture of these two regions is known as the fall line. It extends from Augusta on the Savannah River through Macon on the Ocmulgee to Columbus on the Chattahoochee River. From Columbus it extends westward into Alabama, crossing the Alabama River just north of Montgomery. In Mississippi the fall line turns north and northeast. The next important point on the line is the Muscle Shoals of the Tennessee River.

The substructure of the coastal plain being of less dense material was quickly eroded, and in each stream that crosses this line one finds falls of varying sizes. The falls are generally of sufficient size to handicap river transportation, and for this reason towns have grown up below the falls. These

[1] *American History and Its Geographical Conditions*, p. 150.

towns were important in early days as ports of transshipment.

Another rather marked difference between the Southern and Central states in the westward movement was due to the direction of the flow of the rivers and streams. In the Central states they had a general east and west flow, while in the South the direction was either south or southeastward. In other words, the paths of western migration were not along the rivers and streams but counter to them. This was true in all cases with the exception of the Savannah River, which was used to a great extent in traveling from Savannah to Augusta. From Augusta the direction of travel most frequently followed was westward or southwestward into the Indian country. The other river of importance in Georgia flowing into the Atlantic was the Altamaha, which was formed by the Oconee and Ocmulgee rivers; but as the direction of its flow was southeastward, it was of little value as a path into the west. In the southwestern part of Georgia is the Apalachicola River, which flows almost due south and is formed by the confluence of the Chattahoochee River and the Flint River. The flow of this river was at right angles to the stream of immigrants into the Indian country. The other rivers of importance in the old Southwest were the Alabama and the Tombigbee, which flowed into the Mobile Bay stimulating traffic between Montgomery and Mobile, and the Pearl River farther west. All of these rivers played minor parts in the opening up of the Southwest as compared with the major parts played by the Ohio and its tributaries.

Other avenues of approach into the vast country inhabited only by Indians should be considered. Even before the coming of the Red Man, the area was inhabited. The wild animals roamed the valleys, grazed in the meadows, and searched out the salt licks. They seemed to be well

INDIAN TRAILS OR TRACES

educated in matters pertaining to road engineering. Thomas Hart Benton in a speech before the Senate on December 16, 1850, said that

there is a class of topographical engineers older than the schools and more unerring than the mathematicians. They are the wild animals—buffalo, elk, deer, antelope, bears—which traverse the forest not by compass but by an instinct which leads them always the right way—to the lowest passes in the mountains, the shallowest fords in the rivers, the richest pastures in the forests, the best salt springs, and the shortest practicable lines between remote points. They travel thousands of miles, have their annual migrations backwards and forwards, and never miss the best and shortest route.[2]

These old trails changed very slowly, being altered only by erosion and climatic shifts. When the Indian came into the country he found it "already covered with them and began using them because they led him to water and to salt licks and other places where the primal necessities—water, food, and material for clothing—could be obtained."[3]

At first the animal trails were the only avenues for penetration into the new country, but soon they became the "media of friendly or hostile communication between the people themselves."[4] Senator Benton continued by saying that after the buffalo road became a war path for the Indian it was later used as "the wagon road of the white man and finally the macadamized or railroad of the scientific man."[5]

One's attention is now turned to the Indian trail, which was the first stage of development after the animal trail. Centuries ago, when the Indians came into the Southwest, they found the country covered with a vast net-work of animal trails. Quite naturally they followed these trails

[2] *Congressional Globe*, XXIII, 57.
[3] William E. Myer, "Indian Trails of the Southeast," *42nd Annual Report, Bureau of American Ethnology*, p. 735.
[4] *Ibid.*
[5] *Congressional Globe*, XXIII, 57.

whenever it was possible. Later when the Indians settled down, many of the trails previously made by the animal were converted into avenues of travel and soon lost their original identity. Along with these they developed a system of trails and paths connecting their villages.

In considering the ancient Indian trail William Edward Myer said that one should "bear in mind the life, habits and surroundings of the Indian. These trails followed the lines of least resistance; they avoided rough, stony ground, briars, and close undergrowth such as is formed by laurel. This was to prevent undue wear on clothing or footgear and to save time."[6]

In the mountains and hill country the trails usually led along the higher ground and ridges where the undergrowth was not so dense and where there were fewer streams to cross. James Adair described some that did not follow the ridges but extended "along the rivers and large creeks, to get a safe passage: and the paths are so steep in many places, that the horses often pitch and rear on end, to scramble up."[7]

The trails along the ridges also afforded good opportunity for sighting game and enemies. These two factors determined to a great extent the location for paths. In times of peace or in friendly country the open and well marked trails could be used, but in the enemy country they were avoided. Instead the Indians took "such courses as would render it hardest for the enemy to detect their presence . . . as bare rocks or similar surfaces on which little or no impression was left, or the beds of streams where their tracks were soon obliterated."[8]

Numerous tribes of Indians resided in the South during the eighteenth century. There were the Creek, Cherokee,

[6] *Op. cit.*, p. 743.
[7] *The History of the American Indians*, p. 228.
[8] Myer, *op. cit.*, p. 743.

Choctaw, and Chickasaw Nations, each a distinct and separate group, having its own tribal organization.

The Creek Indians were united in a confederation which formed the largest division of the Muskhogean family. They inhabited the southern part of Alabama and Georgia. As that section of the country had numerous streams and creeks, the English called them the Creek Indians. In early historic times, the Creeks occupied the greater portion of Alabama and Georgia, residing chiefly on the Coosa and Tallapoosa rivers, the two largest tributaries of the Alabama River, and also on the Flint and Chattahoochee rivers.[9]

The Creek Indians were divided geographically into two groups, the Upper Creek and the Lower Creek towns. The Upper Creek towns were situated on the Coosa and Tallapoosa rivers in Alabama, while the Lower Creek towns were on the Chattahoochee River south of the fall line and along the Alabama-Georgia border.

The early statistics of the Creek population are based on mere estimates. There is no way to ascertain definitely the numerical relation which the mixed bloods held to the full bloods.

In the last quarter of the 18th Century, the Creek population may have been about 20,000, occupying from 40 to 60 towns. Knox in 1789[10] estimated them at 6,000 warriors, or a total of 24,000 inhabitants in 100 towns; but these evidently included the Seminole of Florida. Bartram, about 1775, credits the whole confederation, exclusive of the Seminole, with 11,000 in 55 towns. Hawkins, in 1785, gave them 5,400 men, representing a total of about 19,000.[11]

The Chickasaws were another important Muskhogean tribe closely related to the Choctaws in language and customs, although the two tribes were mutually hostile. Their

---

[9] Frederick Webb Hodge, *Handbook of American Indians*, I, 362; cf. *American State Papers, Indian Affairs*, I, 15.
[10] *Ibid.* [11] Hodge, *op. cit.*, p. 364.

territory was situated in northern Mississippi with the Chickasaw Bluffs (now the site of Memphis, Tennessee) as their principal landing place. The population estimates vary widely, "those of the 18th Century ranging from 2,000 to nearly 6,000."[12]

Although the Cherokee Indians resided primarily within the mountainous country, the immigrant came in contact with them while passing over the Upper Trading Path. They were a powerful, detached tribe of the Iroquoian family, formerly holding the whole mountain region of the South Alleghanies. Geographically their settlements were in two groups: those situated east of the mountains and those situated in a section known as "over-the-hill," from which they take the name of "over-the-hill" settlements.

With the exception of an estimate in 1730, which placed the population at 20,000, "most of these up to a recent period gave them 12,000 to 14,000, and in 1759 they were computed at only 7,500. The majority of early estimates are probably too low, as the Cherokee occupied so extensive a territory that only a part of them came in contact with the whites."[13]

The region inhabited by the Choctaw and Chickasaw Indians lay to the west of the Creek Nation. The Choctaws were an important tribe of the Muskhogean stock, occupying middle and southern Mississippi. They were preëminently the agriculturalists of the southern Indians. "The population of the tribe when it first came into relations with the French, about the year 1700, has been estimated at from 15,000 to 20,000."[14]

During the intervals of peace, commerce was widespread among the Indians. The objects of trade passed from hand to hand within a tribe, then between tribes thus linking far remote sections. Lafitau, the Jesuit Father, described the barter trade as it existed in 1710:

[12] *Ibid.*, p. 261.   [13] *Ibid.*, p. 247.   [14] *Ibid.*, p. 289.

The savage nations always trade with one another. Their commerce is, like that of the ancients, a simple exchange of wares. Each has something particular which the others have not, and the traffic makes these things circulate among them. Their wares are grain, porcelain (wampum), furs, robes, tobacco, mats, canoes, work made of moose or buffalo hair and porcupine quills, cotton-beds, domestic utensils—in a word, all sorts of necessities of life required by them.[15]

It was over the trading paths of the Indians that Narvaez, De Vaca, De Soto, and De Luna advanced during the middle of the sixteenth century. They proceeded into the country, passing in a day's journey from one village to another, being directed by native guides. "It is noticeable that these explorers frequently mention the fact that there was no road, and it may well be assumed in consequence, that after their first experiences in mountain and plain they quickly learned to distinguish the indications of an Indian trail and to take advantage of it."[16]

Travel varied in its ease according to the section traversed. In the lowlands they met with many hardships, swamps, wide rivers, and narrow rivers with adjacent bog land. These had to be crossed, and the Spaniards were not so agile in fording streams as were the natives, therefore it was necessary to provide a means. For this purpose they employed either a bridge which varied in complexity according to the width of the stream, or a piragua for rivers too broad to be bridged.

The simplest form of bridge used by the Indian and the Spaniard was a single tree felled so that it would span the creek. For the native this was sufficient, but the European was not so clever in crossing on a single log; his shoe would not cling to the round surface as would the moccasined or

[15] Myer, *op. cit.*, p. 737.
[16] Woodbury Lowery, *The Spanish Settlements within the Present Limits of the United States, 1513-1561*, p. 54.

bare foot of the Indian. The width of the bridges varied, two to four logs being lashed together.[17] Several instances are noted where two bridges were built to facilitate quick movement across a stream. At many places they had great difficulty in gaining the opposite shores because of the strong current. One of the methods used was ingenious. The Spaniards placed

> the horses in the river in line, head and tail, and they were as steady as they could be, and on each one his master, and they received the force of the stream, and on the lower side, where the water was not so violent, the (foot) soldiers forded, and holding on to the tail and stirrup, breast-pieces, and manes, one after the other. And in this way the whole army got across very well.[18]

Many of the streams were not only swift but were wide, too wide to be spanned by a log bridge. In this event other means were necessary; the most popular being the piragua or "dug-out."[19] In the chronicle of Biedma are descriptions of piraguas that had the capacity for carrying "sixty or seventy men and five or six horses."[20] Further on he stated that it took twenty-seven or twenty-eight days to construct four piraguas of this size.[21] For that type of craft, which was constructed from a tree trunk, a fallen log was selected. It was necessary that it be entirely sound and having lain awhile would have been somewhat seasoned.

Sometimes a standing tree was chosen by the Indians and felled by means of hatchets or fire. A section of the trunk from fifteen to thirty feet long and about three feet in diameter was

---

[17] E. G. Bourne, *Narratives of the Career of Hernando de Soto*, I (Elvas narrative), 39, 40, 41, 46, 54, 121; II (Ranjel narrative), 63, 70, 71, 72, 77, 79, 84, 85, 139; II (Biedma narrative), 6, 10; Theodore Maynard, *De Soto and the Conquistadores*, p. 170.

[18] Bourne, *op. cit.*, II (Ranjel narrative), 109; Maynard, *op. cit.*, pp. 170, 200.

[19] Bourne, *op. cit.*, II (Biedma narrative), 9, 22, 26; I (Elvas narrative). 52, 99, 112, 114, 115.

[20] *Ibid.*, II (Biedma narrative), 26.

[21] *Ibid.*

then cut out and elevated from the ground, for convenience in carrying on the work. The log was shaped and hollowed by fire and cutting implements; and a very strong and serviceable, though rough and slow moving craft was obtained.[22]

Francis Moore, in 1735, described piraguas as being "long flat-bottom'd Boats, carrying from 20 to 35 tons. They have a kind of a Forecastle and a cabbin; but the rest open, and no deck. They have two masts, which they can strike, and sails like Schooners. They row generally with two oars only"; but occasionally more are used.[23] This type of craft was a modification of the original piragua but still carried the name.

There was some confusion in the use of names. Some authorities called the boats used "piraguas," while others referred to them as "barges" or "rafts." The raft seems to have been of entirely different construction. One of these rafts, Elvas described as being built of "cane and dried wood."[24] On March 5, 1540, a boat was constructed by de Soto's army, and in Ranjel's account it was called a "barge,"[25] but in Elvas' account the name "piragua" was applied.[26] It is apparent that the names have been used interchangeably and both refer to a hollowed-out trunk of a tree. Certain barges improved upon the single "dug-out." A piragua was cut into two lengthwise sections and a flat bottom of planking was inserted thus increasing the breadth.[27] A fact that seemed to verify this was given by Elvas, who stated that they wanted to "cut down trees for sawing out planks to build a barge."[28]

[22] Seymour Dunbar, *A History of Travel in America*, I, 21.
[23] *A Voyage to Georgia, begun in the Year 1735*, p. 49.
[24] Bourne, *op. cit.*, I (Elvas narrative), 89; also cf. "Narrative of Nunez Cabeca de Vaca," *Spanish Explorers in the Southern United States*, p. 25.
[25] Bourne, *op. cit.*, II (Ranjel narrative), 83.
[26] *Ibid.*, I (Elvas narrative), 52.
[27] *Encyclopaedia Britannica*, 14th ed., XVII, 953.
[28] Bourne, *op. cit.*, I (Elvas narrative), 112.

The streams were so swift that they had difficulty even when they used a piragua. Ranjel in his narrative described the method they used in combatting a rapid current. He stated that

> they took the chains in which they were bringing the Indians, and with some 'S' hooks of iron, fastened them together and made one chain of them all. They fastened one end of the chain to one bank and the other to another in order to take over the barge, and the current was so strong that the chain broke twice. Seeing this, they fastened many ropes together and made of them two, and they fastened one to the stern and the other to the bow and drawing the barge first one way and then the other, they got the people and the baggage across.[29]

Thus it can be seen that travel was slow for the early white man when he came into the old Southwest. He had to follow the Indian trails and go where they might lead him. At first he was interested only in gold and later he became interested in trade.

So up and down these old trails he went in search of Indians that he might trade with, and it was not long before these half hidden trails became avenues of commerce. C. F. Volney described one of these paths of commerce: "Everywhere I found the roads, or, rather paths, bordered and overshadowed with coppices or tall trees; the silence and sameness of which, the soil in some places parched up, in others marshy, trees fallen through age, or blown down by storms and rotting on the ground,"[30] thus in every way giving the impression of desolation. This appearance of desolation was deceptive for the traders as they went silently through the forests.

They were often heard as distinctly in the breaking of twigs or in their muffled tread by the alert ears of the Indian as the musl-

---

[29] *Ibid.*, II (Ranjel narrative), 83.
[30] *View of the Climate and Soil of the United States*, pp. 7, 8.

cal voices of these venders are heard in the city. And the places where these traders put down their cheap trinkets before their dusky patrons grew into trading-posts, prophetic of future cities and towns.[31]

James Adair described a method employed in crossing deep rivers by the early traders about the year 1775:

When we expect high rivers, each company of traders carry a canoe, made of tanned leather, the sides overlapped about three fingers breadth, and well sewed with three seams. Around the gunnels, which are made of sapplings, are strong loop-holes, for large deerskin strings to hang down both sides; with two of these, is securely tied to the stem and stern, a well-shaped sappling, for a keel, and in like manner the ribs. Thus, they usually rig out a canoe, fit to carry over ten horse loads at once, in the space of half an hour; the apparatus is afterwards commonly hidden with great care, on the opposite short. Few take the trouble to paddle the canoe; for, as they are commonly hardy and also of an amphibious nature,[32] they usually jump into the river with their leather barge ahead of them, and thrust it through the deep part of the water, to the opposite shore. When we ride only with a few luggage-horses as was our case at Sip-se, or 'Popular,' the above mentioned high-swelled river, we made a frame of dry pines, which we tie together with strong vines, well twisted; when we have raised it to be sufficiently buoyant, we load and paddle it across the stillest part of the water we can conveniently find, and afterwards swim our horses together, we keeping at a little distance below them.[33]

It was in this manner that the early explorers followed the traces of the Indians through the forests, which at that time covered the southern slopes of the Appalachian Mountains as well as the territory between the mountains and the Gulf of Mexico. This travel was sporadic, not regular or

[31] John Finley, *The French in the Heart of America*, p. 178.
[32] Cf. *Niles' Weekly Register*, X (1816), 314.
[33] Adair, *op. cit.*, p. 272; also cf. p. 325.

organized, and continued to be so until the trading companies and the private traders had an opportunity to evaluate the Indian trade and prepare to take advantage of it. The well defined trading path was the result of this activity.

From the geographical locations of the tribes it may be seen that the Indians primarily involved in the white man's use of their trading paths were the Creeks and the Choctaws. It was their territory that had to be crossed and their streams that required either bridges or ferries to facilitate movement into the west. Their native home was being made the property of everyone; the rights of the Indian were being ignored.

The condition of mutual hostility between the red man and the white did not develop in a day but was the result of many years of contacts of one race with the other. As a matter of fact, the earliest date that may be ascribed to the first hints of hostility was that of the landing of De Soto at Tampa Bay, May, 1539. From that time on relations became more and more involved.

The names of De Soto, De Leon, De Luna, and De Vaca all bring to mind Indian oppression. They were gentlemen adventurers of Spain in search of wealth and eternal youth. Theirs was not the desire to help the Indian but to use him as a means to an end. They were in need of pack animals and slaves, and the Indians filled this place. As a result of this period of dominance the Indian began to think of the white man as a "foreign devil." He made no distinctions; they were all the same in his sight. The white man had never been willing to treat with the Indian on an equal basis. This belief was firmly rooted, and it was only after many years that the Indian was moved to think differently of the new comer. The French had a part in this change, for they were interested in the Indian and his welfare. The Church father and the trader went hand in hand into the

Indian village, lived there and looked after their well being. After living with them for years, the French won the confidence of the Indian and progress was made toward reconciliation. If the French could have exerted their influence over all the area affected by the "conquistadore," the background of American penetration would have been much different. But that was not the case, for the Creek Indian did not forget the Spaniard and his methods of conquest.

CHAPTER II
TRADING PATHS OF THE EARLY SETTLERS

BEFORE 1733, the date James Oglethorpe founded Savannah, the Indian trade in the South was centered at Charleston, South Carolina. The trading paths led from Charleston to the "forked country"; that is, the country in the fork formed by the Flint and the Chattahoochee Rivers. Paths also led to the "over-the-hill" towns of the Cherokees.[1]

During the first quarter of the eighteenth century both France and Spain tried to extend their influence among the Indians living in the Mississippi Valley. "In 1730 a vigorous effort was made to counteract the French influence among the Indians of the hill country by sending Sir Alexander Cuming on a dangerous but successful mission to the Cherokees, which resulted in their acknowledging the English supremacy and promising the monopoly of their trade."[2]

Even before the opening of the eighteenth century Governor Nicholson of Maryland foresaw the dangerous consequence which would follow the completion of La Salle's project and "recommended that the Southern colonies extend their trading posts westward and at least prevent the Indians from going over in a body to the French."[3] It came as a word of warning to some, but to the greater number it was a note of encouragement. Many of them needed reinforcements, and this recommendation gave them reassurance. The advance of the trading frontier of Charleston was notable since her traders were deprived of the natural factor of most influence in the expansion of New France, the ad-

[1] Verner W. Crane, "The Tennessee River as the Road to Carolina," *Mississippi Valley Historical Review*, III (1916-1917), 9.
[2] Evarts Boutell Greene, *Provincial America, 1690-1740*, p. 251.
[3] Crane, *op. cit.*, p. 11.

vantage of water routes. One of their paths led from Charleston overland by way of the Creek villages on the Oconee, the Ocmulgee, the Chattahoochee, and the forks of the Alabama, to the settlements of the Chickasaws. This was a land journey all the way, which, though it avoided the greatest obstacle to the expansion of the northern colonies, the mountain barrier, crossed many large rivers and traversed a virgin forest.

The Indian trade was the most important factor which led men to penetrate the wilderness. Before the establishment of Savannah this trade was the most lucrative branch of commerce carried on in South Carolina. "It had developed with a rapidity and on a scale scarcely paralleled in any other English colony, so that by 1699, in which year Charles Town exported more than sixty-five thousand deerskins besides a considerable quantity of beaver and many Indian slaves, her traders had reached and even passed the Mississippi in their journey."[4]

Transportation naturally figured in trade relations between the seaboard and the valley. The requirements of the Indian trader were generally met by the traders themselves without any call upon the government or upon the planter for assistance.

In fact, the trading routes supplied avenues to the commonwealths at later times without the trouble of initial location by the authorities. Except where rivers were available, Indian traders used pack-horses in trains for their traffic. Since no wheeled vehicles were used, there was no need of anything more than trails; and there was no demand for bridges and causeways sufficient to secure their construction. The routes of the Indian traders were mere bridle-paths through the wilderness. In view of the boggy character of most of the bottom lands and the general disadvantages of crossing large water-courses, these paths usually followed the water sheds as far as possible. When routes

[4] *Ibid.*, p. 9.

necessarily crossed river valleys, they were so located as to avoid steep ascents and to cross streams at points where the banks were firm.[5]

William Bartram gave an interesting picture of a trader on the path somewhere in Georgia.

They seldom decamp until the sun is high and hot; each one having a whip made of the toughest cow-skin, they start all at once, the horses having ranged themselves in regular Indian file, the veteran in the van, and the younger in the rear; then the chief drives with the crack of his whip, and a whoop or shriek, which rings through the forest and plains, speaks in Indian, commanding them to proceed, which is repeated by all the company, then we start at once, keeping up a brisk and constant trot, which is incessantly urged and continued as long as the miserable creatures are able to move forward; then come to camp. . . .[6]

Savannah was settled in February, 1733, and from that month dates a new period in Indian trade. The center of trading activities gradually shifted from Charleston to Savannah. Each person who intended to trade with the Indians was required to secure a license which designated the area in which he could operate. It was necessary for the "traders to renew their licenses at Savannah yearly in March, April, May, or June, except the traders with the Chickasaws, who" were "to renew theirs every 18 months."[7] The ordinances also stated "that all such Persons as shall intend to Trade to the Nations of Indians called Chickesaws shall not Trade Traffick or Barter with any Indian or Indians in their way to the said Nations called Chickesaws. . . ."[8] In addi-

[5] C. E. MacGill, *History of Transportation in the United States before 1860*, pp. 252, 253.
[6] *Travels through North and South Carolina, East and West Florida*, . . . , pp. 438, 439.
[7] *Colonial Records of Georgia*, I, 38; IV, 166, 358, 362, 369, 568, 578, 585; supplement to IV, 154, 155, 183; XVIII, 247-49, 703-5; XIII, 287, 296; XXII (pt. II), 247.
[8] *Ibid.*, I, 38, 39.

tion "every Trader going to the Creeks to Trade shall be Obliged to pass both going and coming by the first Fort Argyll or by such other Fort or Forts as shall from time to time be appointed by the Common Council. . . ."[9] A penalty was affixed to prevent illegal trading. The ordinances stated that "if any Person or Persons whatsoever (other than such as duly Obtain Licenses . . .) shall directly or indirectly Visit frequent haunt Trade to Traffic or Barter with any Indian or Indians within the said Province of Georgia all and every such Offender or Offenders shall for every such Offence Forfeit One hundred pounds sterling. . . ."[10] Such conditions continued for about two years and in 1735, Captain Patrick Mackey was sent over as Agent for Indian Affairs in the Colony of Georgia.[11] In a communication dated May 28, 1735, addressed to a Mr. Jones, an Indian trader, Captain Mackey said that

> I found on my arrival here the Trade of this Nation in very great disorder, which I imputed to the Numbers Licensed to Trade and which as Governed could not afford a Living for Some Traders, which was the Reason they were guilty of unfair Practices. I have Regulated the Trade a little, and Reduc'd the Number of Traders and that you may not disappoint yourself, I am Sorry I must tell you that you are not in the Number of those continued Therefore you are to withdraw yourself & Effects with all Convenient Diligence from this Nation. . . .[12]

James Oglethorpe received a letter dated July 3, 1736, in which the needs of Savannah were stressed. More supplies were needed there to equip the Indians for their winter hunt. In the words of the communication:

> The Indian Traders which are come here this year for there Licenses having brought down a Considerable Quantity of Leather to the Value of 14 or 15,000 Sterling which they designed

[9] *Ibid.*, p. 40.
[10] *Ibid.*, p. 32.
[11] *Ibid.*, XXI, 3.
[12] *Ibid.*, pp. 10, 11.

to have sold here if they Could have been provided with Goods for the next winter's Hunt but there being no Goods proper for them in Town but a Small Quantity that I had they were obliged to Carry there Leather to Chas Town which they will always be Obliged to do if they Cannot provide themselvs with Goods here by which the Settlers here will lose the Benefit his Majesty & the Honble the Trustees designed for this Infant Colony. . . . If there Honours will be pleased to Give there Assistance so as to gett the Indian Trade settled here it will be a very great Advantage to the whole private people settled in this Colony & also to the Publick . . . & when this Trade is once fixed in a place it will not be soon removed the Most part of the Traders being now inclinable to remove all there Effects from Carolina & Settle intirely in this Collony if there be a prospect of there being provided in Goods here.[13]

The shifting of trade from Charleston to Savannah is exemplified by one trader who "had last Year taken Licence from Carolina, doubting he was not well warranted from thence to trade in those Towns therein named; now threw it up, and desired a Licence might be granted him from Georgia."[14]

Savannah was the center from which paths radiated. All of them had a general westward direction supplemented by those leading to St. Augustine to the southwest and the one to Augusta and the Cherokee nation which went in a northwestward direction. A statement was made in 1740 in regard to the line of communication between Augusta and Savannah.

The Great Value of this Town of Augusta occasioned the General [Oglethorpe] to have a Path marked out, through the Woods, from thence to Old Ebenezer; and the Cherokee Indians have marked out one from thence to their Nation, so that Horsemen now can ride from the Town of Savannah to the Nation of the

[13] *Ibid.*, XXI, 186, 187; also cf. p. 175.
[14] *Ibid.*, IV, 578.

Cherokees, and any other of the Indian Nations, all on the Georgia Side of the River; but there are some bad Places which ought to be causewayed and made good, and which the General says he has not yet Capacity to do. This Road begins to be frequented, and will every Day be more and more so, and by it the Cherokee Indians can at any Time come down to our Assistance.[15]

Another system of trails and paths converged at Augusta. A glance at the military map prepared by the British Government for the use of their troops during the Revolutionary War will be sufficient to attest the fact. Their trail system was comparable to our road system. Some of the traders chose to come into Augusta and then either travel down the Savannah River to Savannah[16] or down the path that had been laid out.[17] Augusta was situated in an important position just below the falls of the Savannah River, and thus would derive much benefit from the fact that small boats had to be conveyed around the falls, and large ships could not go upstream any farther. Roger Lacy settled the town and built a fort there in 1739.[18] Points of transshipment are always likely locations for settlements. There are at least three types of transshipment: (1), from trail to river crafts; (2), from small river crafts to larger ones below the fall line; (3), from large river crafts or from the trail to sea-going vessels. Augusta was so situated that it could take advantage of the first two, while Savannah enjoyed the benefit of the third type. These factors were important where goods were transported by pack-trains and river crafts.

The trail systems of Savannah and Augusta were gradually improved as the trade warranted it. Traders were sent

[15] *Ibid.*, p. 667.
[16] *Ibid.*, pp. 550, 552; supplement to IV, 81, 85.
[17] *Ibid.*, IV, 82, 133, 161, 202, 203; supplement to IV, 134.
[18] *Ibid.*, XXII (pt. II), 277.

into all the Indian nations[19] to represent the British interests and to offset the French and Spanish influences. In 1739 James Oglethorpe wrote to the Trustees of the Colony of Georgia emphasizing conditions in regard to these influences. "The French have attacked ye Carolina Indians, and the Spanish have invaded us, I wish it may not be resolved between them to root ye English out of America. We here are resolved to dye hard, and will not lose one inch of ground without fighting, but we cannot do Impossibilities."[20] At another time he wrote that "this Province is now in an especial manner become a Frontier against the Enemy (for wch our Neighbors of Carolina ought to show a kinder regard to us). . . ."[21]

To the west, beyond the nations of the Cherokees and the Creeks, were the Choctaws, whose friendship and trade were desired and needed. In a communication dated July 20, 1738, the situation was outlined for the benefit of those in control in London.

I beg leave further to observe to Your Lordships that if a Peace & Commerce can be Effected & maintained with the whole Chactow Nation. How great an Addition of Strength his Majesty's Subjects will have to withstand their Enemys, as well as the enlarging & extending of the Trade for Skins & ffurrs, which may in a little time require double the quantity of British Goods such as Diffils, Strouds, Broadcloth, Guns, Powder, Bullets &c^a to supply that numerous People: And besides these Advantages in Case of a War with the French they can have no Assistance from the Chactaws against the English. . . . But the French at Mobile & near the Mississippi River have no other Indians, but the

---

[19] *Ibid.*, IV, 319, 372, 501, 550, 563, 565, 585; supplement to IV, 55, 85, 127, 128, 131; XIII, 225, 226, 486, 515; XXII (pt. I), 230; XXII (pt. II), 242, 253, 483; XXVI, 212, 279, 389, 402, 404; Philip M. Hamer, "John Stuart's Indian Policy during the Early Months of the American Revolution," *Mississippi Valley Historical Review*, XVII (1930), 360.

[20] *Colonial Records of Georgia*, XXII (pt. II), 267.

[21] *Ibid.*, p. 211.

Chactaws whom they could make use of against the English and the Indians in Amity with them. . . . Your Lordships will immediately observe that the Chactaws by their Situation, if they are gain'd from the French will be able to cut off all Communication between Canada and Louisiana."[22]

In 1762 John Stuart "was appointed superintendent of Indian affairs for the southern department of North America, succeeding in that office Edmond Atkins, recently deceased."[23] Immediately upon taking over the office, John Stuart began to reorganize the Indian affairs, since the stability of the South depended greatly upon the relations of the colonists with the Indians. It seemed that the colony of Georgia, with its Board of Trustees, was able to handle the situation better than had the Traders from Carolina. James Oglethorpe wrote that "they [the Cherokee Indians] called them [the Trustees] the Preservers of their Nation, as they did the Carolina Traders, the Destroyers of it."[24]

Trouble had arisen in many localities over the question of whether Georgia or South Carolina should exercise authority. Numerous instances are recorded of Carolina traders residing within the limits of Georgia.[25] The sovereignty of these two colonies again clashed when the government of Carolina sent a constable to the Creek Nation to execute a warrant without the approval of the authorities of Georgia.[26] As a form of reprisal Joseph Ottolenghe and Noble Wimberly Jones were appointed to draw up a bill and present it to the Assembly of Georgia placing "a Duty on Deer Skins and ffurrs exported from this Province to South Carolina."[27]

With points of variance so numerous a general reorganization of trading relations was needed. John Stuart's plan

[22] *Ibid.*, XXII (pt. I), 213, 214; also cf. XIII, 300, 436, 440.
[23] Hamer, *op. cit.*, p. 351.
[24] *Colonial Records of Georgia*, XXII (pt. II), 248.
[25] *Ibid.*, supplement to IV, 154.
[26] *Ibid.*, XXVII, 398, 407, 408.   [27] *Ibid.*, XIII, 311, 312.

was to have a set of officers stationed with each major Indian group. His recommendation was as follows:

One sett of Officers will be Sufficient for the Small Nations on the Lakes Pontchartrain, Maurepas and the Eastern Bank of the Mississippi, who I humbly propose shall reside at Point Iberville where it is proposed to establish a Post; One sett of Officers for the Chactaw Nations, to reside at Tombeckby, where there are very good Accommodations; one sett in the Chickasaw Nation, and on Sett to reside at Fort De Chartes, in the Illinois Nation; as the Upper and Lower Creeks consider them Selves in Many respects as different people and live at a Distance from each Other. I am of Opinion that two Setts of Officers will be Necessary, one to reside at Fort Apalache the other at the Albama Fort, Two setts of Officers will likewise be necessary for the Cherokee Nation, the Lower and Over-Hill Settlements of which are 160 miles distant, the Officers for the Upper Cherokees to reside at Chotee, those for the Lower at Fort Prince George; as the Catawbas, Lower Chickasaws Near Augusta Tuscaroras in North Carolina Notteways and Samponys in Virginia live among our Settlements and are immediately under the Eye of Government the Expence of Officers for them well may be saved, except an Armourer for the Catawbas and One for the Tuscaroras.[28]

According to his organization the officers would conduct "all Talks and Transactions of a public Nature" and "no provincial agents" were to be "sent into the Indian Nations from any of the Provinces."[29] In addition he wanted to change the method of issuing trading licenses. He proposed "that the power of granting Licenses be vested in the Superintendent; that a certain limited number of Traders be licensed. . . ."[30] Though the plan was criticised by many

[28] "Observations of John Stuart," *American Historical Review*, XX (1915), 819-20; also cf. James Grant, "Gov. James Grant to the Board of Trade," *American Historical Review*, XX (1915), 827-31.

[29] Stuart, *op. cit.*, p. 820.

[30] *Ibid.*; *Georgia Gazette*, 1767, No. 205; 1768, No. 230; Adair, *op. cit.*, p. 366.

people, it seemed at least to be constructive and applicable to the situation. With a better internal organization peace would be more certain and trade would prosper, for without trade and intercourse the paths would grow up from disuse and all the work previously done would be of no value.

During the American Revolution an interesting communication was sent to the Creek Indians from St. Augustine informing them that "there is an unhappy Dispute between the People of England and the white People of America, which however cannot Affect you, as you can be supplied with Necessaries from Pensacola Mobille and this place—where the people live like Brothers and enjoy Peace, and it is not the Intention of Either Party to hurt or Molest you. . . ."[31]

The following table gives an idea of the value of the trade carried on through the port of Savannah, and it must be borne in mind that the products exported from this town had to be brought in from the hinterland over the system of paths already discussed.

Year	Total Exports
1749	$ 10,000
1750	8,897
1753	74,785
1763	193,395
1773	379,422
1786	321,377
1796	501,383
1800	2,155,982
1818	14,183,113
1821	6,132,862[32]

[31] Hamer, *op. cit.*, p. 359.
[32] F. D. Lee and J. L. Agnew, *Historical Record of the City of Savannah*, p. 137.

Mobile, on the Mobile Bay, was also a trading center during the eighteenth and early nineteenth centuries. Mobile, like Savannah, was situated at the point of transshipment from river crafts to ocean going vessels. Almost all of the trade that came into this center came by water, the Tombigbee and the Alabama Rivers being routes used from the hinterland. Along with and in connection with these river routes were the land routes. On the east they led from the Upper and Lower Creek Nations and on the west from the Chickasaw and Choctaw Nations.

Two letters written by gentlemen in Mobile described early trading conditions there. The first was dated October, 1763.

... The situation (of Mobile) is well calculated for Indian trade, the town pleasantly situated on the river Mobille, which divides in two branches, each extending near the middle of the Choctaw and Creek Nations, and I am informed that Boats drawing three feet may go all seasons of the year; I believe in time we shall have a very considerable trade with the Indians by the change of civil government; the inhabitants do not seem to like an English military government.[33]

The second letter was dated about a month later and enlarged upon the former statements. The gentleman who wrote this letter had been in Pensacola and had gone to Mobile.

By land from Pensacola to Mobille is two days journey, but the road bad, there being a wide river and several creeks to cross: By water the distance is about 27 leagues, viz., from town to sea 3, from that to the point of Mobille 14, and from thence to the town 10. ... This town [Mobile] consists of only a few straggling houses, mostly stockaded for fear of the Indians, some of them brick, but has a very good regular built brick fort, with a ditch, covered way, and glacis, which the French call Conde,

[33] *Georgia Gazette,* 1763, No. 35.

where on they had mounted 38 pieces of cannon. . . . No place in the universe can be better situated for the Indian trade than this is, as there is water carriage into the heart of the Creek, Chickasaw, and Choctaw Nations, which last is more numerous than we imagined. . . . From this to New Orleans the distance is about 70 leagues, viz., to Isle Dauphin the entrance of the harbour 10, thence to the mouth of the Mississippi 25, and from that to New Orleans 35, there is also an inland passage through the lakes for small crafts, but no road by land. The trade of Pensacola and Mobile hitherto is not worth mentioning."[34]

Trade at Mobile continued to be profitable as is evidenced by the remarks of Thomas Hutchins: "There is a considerable Indian trade carried on here. Mobille, when in possession of his Britannic Majesty, sent yearly to London, skins and furs amounting from 12 to 15,000 pounds sterling: it was then the only staple commodity in this part of the province."[35] In the years that followed there was more diversification in products exchanged. Originally the only people living in the territory with whom the white people might trade were the Indians with their limited wares; then the settler came in and produced a wider variety of articles that were acceptable at the market.

Before the Revolution the control of the fur trade was shifting from Savannah to Mobile and Pensacola. "This tendency was strengthened by the fact that most of the British Indian agents and traders were loyalists during the Revolution and that many of them took refuge in East and West Florida."[36] During the period the supplies destined for the Indians and shipped by way of Charleston and Savannah had been cut off and the trade thrown into the

[34] *Ibid.*, 1764, No. 45.
[35] *An Historical Narrative and Topographical Description of Louisiana, and West-Florida*, p. 70.
[36] Arthur Preston Whitaker, *The Spanish-American Frontier: 1783-1795*, p. 25.

hands of the loyal Britons residing in Pensacola, Mobile, and St. Augustine. As the war came to a close it was necessary to decide who should have the Indian trade, Spain or the United States, both former enemies of Great Britain. Spain seemed to be the one favored, for

Spanish influence was paramount among the Southern Indians, whose trade was falling more and more into the hands of Panton, Leslie and Company. The Company with stores at St. Mark's, Pensacola, and Mobile, and with a business whose capital value in 1794 was estimated by Panton and Carondelet at $400,000, seemed most favorably situated to engross the fur trade as it retreated westward in the face of the advancing American and Spanish frontiers.[37]

The settlers in the Cumberland Valley were trying to divert the fur trade from Mobile and Pensacola to Nashville and the projected post at Chickasaw Bluffs.[38] This was a natural desire, but its fulfillment was not simple. Nashville and the Chickasaw Bluffs were focal points for certain areas, but Mobile controlled a much larger section. The systems of the Alabama and Tombigbee Rivers formed natural avenues of approach, and the numerous trading paths increased their importance. Arthur Preston Whitaker said that "economically the Southern fur trade was a doubtful value, for it was highly speculative, and while the profits were often large the risks were always great."[39]

As the years passed, new products such as cotton and lumber were brought into the market. They were bulky, and cheap transportation was necessary. The river systems and their connecting roadways were of greatest assistance; therefore, the major part of the trade was carried on in Mobile and New Orleans.

The two cities were situated on streams that flowed out

[37] *Ibid.*, p. 177.
[38] *Ibid.*, pp. 59, 60.   [39] *Ibid.*, p. 26.

of the hinterland rather than through it, as did some of the streams farther east. A letter from Mobile dated November 6, 1824, described trading conditions there: "This city, but as yesterday, was a place of no importance—and the business transacted therein, for the last two or three years, has astonished every one."[40] The letter contained in tabular form the exports of cotton, sawed lumber, and staves, from the Fort of Mobile during the year ending September 30, 1824.

Foreign

Liverpool	8,778 bales of cotton
Glascow	352 bales of cotton
Greenock	463 bales of cotton
France	717 bales of cotton
Total	10,310 bales of cotton

Coastwise

Boston	967 bales of cotton
New York	14,999 bales of cotton
Philadelphia	352 bales of cotton
New Orleans	13,094 bales of cotton
Other Ports	460 bales of cotton
Total	29,872 bales of cotton

Recapitulation

	Cotton	Lumber	Staves
Foreign	10,310 bales	790,802 ft.	264,250
Coastwise	29,872 bales	127,000 ft.	342,304
Total	40,182 bales	917,802 ft.	606,554
From Blakely	4,742 bales		

Total from
  Mobile Bay   44,924 bales
Exports during the year ending September 30, 1823
          44,061 bales   612,100 ft.   437,139[41]

[40] *Niles' Weekly Register*, XXVII (1824-25), 149.
[41] *Ibid.*, XXVII (1824-25), 149.

Mobile was destined to become a large shipping port because of its well developed back-country made accessible by a correlated system of roads and waterways. A trading town was dependent upon transportation facilities since the articles that were to be exchanged had to be collected and brought in to the market or assembled for a foreign market.

Another city in a similar situation was New Orleans, which has always been an important trading center, located near the mouth of the Mississippi River. In 1717 it was said to be forty leagues up the river.[42]

There existed in New Orleans an international situation not unlike the problem in Georgia, though the sides were reversed. The French were in control of Louisiana and were fearful of English advances, which they attempted to offset whenever it was possible.[43] They had a good philosophy of colonizing and trading, which was expressed in a report from Paris: "the only means of retaining them and populating this colony is to buy from the inhabitants everything that the country is in a position to produce, without exception and at a reasonable price which could be reduced subsequently."[44]

With such a policy a brisk trade sprang up with the people living in the Mississippi Valley. The people of New Orleans were "concerned with the trade in the skins of buffaloes, cows, stags, does, bears, roebucks, panthers, wolves, and other sorts of small pelts that are very abundant in this continent."[45]

A price list published in 1716 in Paris gives an idea of the nature of the trade in this section:

[42] *Mississippi Provincial Archives*, II, 253.
[43] *Ibid.*, pp. 23-25, 39, 41, 64, 69.
[44] *Ibid.*, p. 221.
[45] *Ibid.*, p. 52.

Peltries	Price of the inhabitants	Offers of the Directors
Cowhides without distinction, some raw and others dressed..... 1½	piastres each	
Merchantable bearskins 1	piastre each	2 livres
Skins of bear cubs.............. 1	livre, 10 sous	1 livre
Deerskins dressed in the Indian manner as parchment........... 1	livre, 10 sous	1, 10
Dressed skins of stags and does... 4	livres	3 livres
Skins of foxes, lynxes and others...36	sous,	
	raccoonskins 10	
Skins of skunks, otters and raccoons	at the ordinary prices	
Lead in bars................... 10	sous per lb.	
Ordinary tallow 10	sous per lb.	
Sassafras root 10	livres per 100 lbs.	Nothing since there is no sale for them[46]
China-root 10	livres per 100 lbs.	
Raw beef 30	livres per 100 lbs.	

In Louisiana there were numerous Indian trails converging at New Orleans, over which the Indians and traders came with their merchandise. One account, written in New Orleans, said that "the Choctaws are coming every day to ask that the Company build a warehouse within reach of them in order to trade for their buffalo, bear, and deer skins. In this they will be obliged to listen to the proposals of the English which they have been unwilling to hear up to the present."[47]

Relations were also established with the Canadians in the upper Mississippi Valley. In a report dated Jan. 30, 1729, there appeared the following statement:

[46] *Ibid.*, p. 225.   [47] *Ibid.*, p. 461.

Several Canadians have come to us from the Illinois who have brought us some beaver skins which have been received and examined by Mr. D'Ausseville who knows all about them. Among these people there were two of good families. They told us that if we would make a treaty with them, they would bring us 20,000 livres worth of beaver skins every year and that if we were willing to take them on the basis on which they were received in Canada, all the Canadians would bring them here.[48]

Pensacola,[49] a Spanish settlement, was another point contacted by the business establishments of New Orleans. This commerce was usually carried on by water, though sometimes it was supplemented by land routes between Mobile and Pensacola. The most important articles of commerce were pelts. The prices paid during the year 1729 were:

Dry beaver skins	34 sous per pound
Fat beaver skins	3 livres per pound
Deer skins	34 sous per pound
Raccoon skins	15 sous each
Dressed merchantable stag and doeskins	5 livres each
Forest wolves	40 sous each
Foxes	40 sous each
Wildcats	40 sous each
Large bear skins	5 livres each
Ordinary merchantable bear skins	3 livres each
Otter-skins, large and dark	4 livres each

John Filson, in his history of Kentucky, said, "I have reason to believe that the time is not far distant when New Orleans will be a great trading city, and perhaps another will be built near Nantchac, at Iberville, that may in time rival its glory."[50] This statement was made during the last few years of the eighteenth century.

After the Revolutionary War, the American government

---

[48] *Ibid.*, p. 619; also cf. p. 664.
[49] *Ibid.*, p. 632.
[50] *The Discovery, Settlement and Present State of Kentucke*, p. 44.

organized the territory inhabited by the Indians into two districts, the northern and the southern. The southern district, according to an early document, "comprehended within its limits all the nations in the territory of the United States who resided southward of the Ohio. . . ."[51] Over this section a superintendent was placed whose duties were numerous and exceedingly trying. It was his duty to carry on negotiations with the Indians, representing as he did the United States Government. Many treaties were made concerning property turned over to the government by the Indians.[52] This subject seemed to have been the most important during the early days of statehood in the South. Nothing else was of any moment until later when the desire to improve the Indian paths prevailed. The date for this can be placed about 1800, for one of the first treaties recorded was one negotiated between the United States and the Chickasaw Indians, dated October 24, 1801.

There had been considerable discussion prior to the treaty concerning the opening of a road through their territory. Henry Dearborn, writing from the War Department to Davie, Wilkinson, and Hawkins, stated his views, which represented the governmental attitude.

It is suggested, that the Indians will oppose our request for opening roads, for the two following reasons: that their cattle and horses will travel too far from home on such roads, and be driven away, and stolen by the white people, who may travel on said road.

To obviate these objections, it may be proper to agree, on the part of the United States, that no white person shall be allowed to travel on the road to Natchez, except as shall have procured passes from our agents at Tennessee and at Natchez, which passes shall be countersigned by the men who may be stationed at the several houses to be established on the roads, and that gates

[51] *American State Papers, Indian Affairs*, I, 14.
[52] *Ibid.*, p. 15; and *passim*.

shall be erected at some of the bridges on that road, and maintained by the United States, to prevent the horses and cattle of the Indians from straying far from home.[53]

It was with this in mind that Benjamin Hawkins and Andrew Pickens, commissioners of the United States, met with the Chickasaws to draw up a treaty of reciprocal advantages and mutual convenience. The outstanding points of the treaty are as follows:

Article I: The Mingo,[54] principal men and warriors of the Chickasaw nation of Indians, give leave and permission to the President of the United States of America, to lay out, open and make a convenient wagon road through their land ... the same shall be a highway for the citizens of the United States, and the Chickasaws. ... The necessary ferries over the water courses crossed by the said road shall be held and deemed to be the property of the Chickasaw nation.

Article II: The commissioners of the United States give to the mingo of the Chickasaws, and deputation of that nation, goods to the value of seven hundred dollars, to compensate him and them. ...

Article III: The commissioners of the United States may, if they deem it advisable, proceed immediately to carry the first article into operation. ...[55]

Under the terms of the treaty the government had the right to open the road through the territory of western Tennessee and northern Mississippi. It was then necessary to negotiate with the Choctaw Indians. The representatives met at Fort Adams on the Mississippi and on December 17,

---

[53] *Ibid.*, p. 650.

[54] The Choctaw and Chickasaw equivalent of the Muskogee *miko*, 'chief,' both words being frequently used by historians and travelers in the Gulf States during the colonial period.

[55] *Indian Affairs, Laws and Treaties*, II, 55, 56; also cf. *American State Papers, Indian Affairs*, I, 648, 649; 7 Stat. 65.

1801 signed a treaty, similar to the one with the Chickasaws in that it gave

their free consent, that a convenient and durable wagonway may be explored, marked, opened and made under orders and instructions of the President of the United States, through their lands to commence at the northern extremity of the settlement of the Mississippi Territory, and to be extended from thence, by such route as may be selected and surveyed. . . .[56]

On December 20, a few days after the treaty was signed, William C. C. Claiborne wrote to James Madison stating his view and one which was typical of the time, especially of those interested in facilitating transportation:

I have at this moment been informed, that the Commissioners of the United States, have concluded a treaty [at Fort Adams] with the Choctaw Nation; the chiefs have consented to the opening of a Road, through their land to Tennessee, but refuse permission to erect houses of accommodation: I presume therefore, that this work will shortly be commenced, and when completed, will no doubt prove a great public convenience.[57]

When, in 1803, France ceded to the United States the province of Louisiana for 80,000,000 francs, the transfer stimulated trade, for there was no question about the river's being open or closed to American trade while the United States controlled the mouth. "With the Spanish and the French removed from the Mississippi, American produce was freed from all foreign interference. The future of New Orleans was assured."[58]

The trading paths were now improved so as to accommodate an established commerce. The figures of 1804-1807 may serve to indicate the character of the trade.

[56] *Indian Affairs, Laws and Treaties*, II, 56; *American State Papers, Indian Affairs*, I, 658; 7 Stat. 66.
[57] *Mississippi Territorial Archives, 1798-1803*, p. 363.
[58] W. F. Galpin, "The Grain Trade of New Orleans, 1804-1814," *Mississippi Valley Historical Review*, XIV (1927), 496.

Flour total ....113,403 bbls.
Corn total .... 43,631 bu.
   Flour from Virginia .... 23,591 bbls.
   Flour from Kentucky .... 35,039 bbls.
   Flour from Pennsylvania .... 47,798 bbls.
   Corn from Kentucky .... 26,180 bu. [59]

With products similar to these a stable trade could be inaugurated, not subject to the variations and irregularities of the fur trade. Yet these articles could not be transported on pack animals but required cheap bulk conveyance, for which the river was best suited and soon became an important factor.

[59] *Ibid.*, pp. 500, 501.

CHAPTER III
IMMIGRATION SOUTH OF THE MOUNTAINS

PROFESSOR Ephraim Douglas Adams quoted a letter dated March, 1823, that he had found in the *Edinburgh Scotsman*. This letter was from America and expressed the feeling of freedom from Old World restraints.

I am here, lord and master of myself and of 100 acres of land—an improvable farm, little trouble to me, good society and a good market, and I think, a fine climate, only a little too hot and dry in summer; the parson gets nothing from me; my state and road taxes and poor rates amount to $25 per annum. I can carry a gun if I choose; I leave my door unlocked at night; and can get snuff for one cent an ounce or a little more.[1]

It was this idea of freedom that permeated all sections of the land and brought immigrants by the hundred.

People thought of the western land as a place of new beginnings, where they might forget their past. Some thought of it as a place where an investment could be made, which would accrue large profits; others could see only the adventure, the glamour, and the uncertainty of the journey into the wilderness. John Randolph wrote in 1813 that

in a few years more, those of us who are alive will move off to Kaintuck or the Mississippi, where corn can be had for six pence a bushel and pork for a penny a pound. I do not wonder at the rage for emigration. What do the bulk of the people get here that they cannot have there for one-fifth the labor in the western country.[2]

That was one view; the other was the one held by the

[1] "The Point of View of the British Traveller in America," *Political Science Quarterly*, XXIX (1914), 250.
[2] Ulrich Bonnell Phillips, *American Negro Slavery*, p. 183.

governments. When the territory south of the Appalachian Mountains was opened and settled, it would act as a protective barrier against the Indians and the Spaniards. A notice to this effect appeared in the *Gentleman's Magazine,* August, 1732. "As towns are established, they will make such a Barrier as will render the Southern Frontier of the British Colonies on the Continent of America, safe from Indians and other enemies."[3]

The first people that came into the southern area were Europeans—Spaniards, Frenchmen, and Englishmen, who sought gold, furs, and homes in the South Atlantic territory. They had left their homes, crossed the Atlantic, and conquered the wilderness. Rich men and poor men, high officials and men from the debtor's prison—all worked side by side, making roads, clearing fields, erecting log cabins—in a word—beginning a new life. Not many years elapsed before the westward movement started. In the lower South the direction was generally southwestward around the mountains.

Preliminaries of the movement into the Gulf Region had begun as early as 1768, when a resident of Pensacola noted that a group of Virginians had been prospecting thereabouts with such favorable results that five of them had applied for a large grant of lands, pledging themselves to bring in a hundred slaves and a large number of cattle.[4]

Populating one section at the expense of another was a problem at this time. William Stork, while traveling in the South in 1766, remarked that

none of the American provinces are so well peopled, as to spare inhabitants; and were any of the inhabitants to the northward disposed to go to Florida, it is, with respect to the migration of families, quite inaccessible by land, for want of roads, and ferrys

[3] *Gentleman's Magazine,* II (1732), 894.
[4] Phillips, *op. cit.,* p. 177.

to pass the several large rivers; and such inhabitants as may be willing to seek a new habitation, cannot afford the expense of conveying themselves and families by sea.[5]

The emigrants moved from the more densely populated sections of Virginia, North and South Carolina, into Georgia and then across the Indian Nation. It was a new country, inadequately mapped, containing many adventures hidden in the deep forests and isolated valleys. Every summit brought a new reality, every stream a new problem, and every forest hid a different enemy. The trails were those made by the Indians and used by the trader, for want of better avenues of penetration. Movement would have been easier and more rapid if accurate and detailed maps had been available, but such was not the case. The few existing maps varied greatly and were notably inaccurate. The cartographers, however, made an effort to include the most valuable information that was available, in order that the emigrant might use the map to the best advantage. J. G. Kohl in an address on early maps said that

Every blue summit of a mountain described by your western settlers and pioneers from a distance, every large or small branch of a new river, every glittering surface of a lake never seen before, was talked of by them around their camp-fires, and gave occasion to all manner of hypothesis and speculation about the end of the lake, about the direction and source of the river, about what those mountains might be, what they might contain, and how they might be connected with the rest. And what those bold pioneers surmised, and what they learned from the Indians in the west, all found echo in the cabinets of the geographers of the East, and you see it conscientiously transferred to their maps, which are changed and corrected a hundred times, . . .[6]

[5] *An Account of East-Florida*, pp. 68, 69; William Stork, *Description of East-Florida*, p. 30.

[6] "Substance of a lecture delivered at the Smithsonian Institute on the collection of Charts and Maps of America," *Annual Report, Smithsonian Institute*, 1856, p. 107.

John James Audubon, a well-informed traveler and a keen observer, described a party of immigrants.

> I think I see them harnessing their horses, and attaching them to their wagons, which are already fitted with bedding, provisions, and the younger children; while on their outside are fastened spinning-wheels and looms, a bucket filled with tar and tallow swings betwixt the hind wheels. Several axes are secured to the bolster, and the feeding trough of the horses contains pots, kettles, and pans. The servant now becomes a driver, riding the near saddled horse, the wife is mounted on another, the worthy husband shoulders his gun, and his sons, clad in plain, substantial home-spun, drive the cattle ahead, and lead the procession, followed by the hounds and other dogs. Their day's journey is short and not agreeable. The cattle, stubborn or wild, frequently, leave the road for the woods giving the travelers much trouble, the harness of the horses here and there gives away, and immediate repair is needed. A basket which has accidentally dropped must be gone after, for nothing that they have can be spared. The roads are bad, and now and then all hands are called to push on the waggon, or prevent it from upsetting. Yet at sunset, they have proceeded perhaps twenty miles. Fatigued, all assemble around the fire, which has been lighted; supper is prepared, and a camp being set up, there they pass the night. Days and weeks pass before they gain the end of their journey. They have crossed both the Carolinas, Georgia, and Alabama. They have been travelling from the beginning of May to that of September, and with heavy hearts they traverse the neighborhood of the Mississippi. But now arrived on the banks of the broad streams, they gaze in amazement on the dark deep woods around them. Boats of various kinds they see gliding downward with the current, while others slowly ascend against it. A few inquiries are made at the nearest dwelling, and assisted by the inhabitants with their boats and canoes, they at once cross the river and select their place of habitation.[7]

[58] W. F. Galpin, "The Grain Trade of New Orleans, 1804-1814," *Mississippi Life and Adventures of Audubon,* ed. by Robert Buchanan, pp. 64, 65.

This picture was typical of the frontier. Along the roads through Georgia, Alabama, and Mississippi people similar to the ones described by Audubon were found. They were interesting people, out on the frontier away from established government, laying the foundations for new states. Among these people the question of communication with New Orleans was always important. When Florida was acquired, it was thought that it would "open a vast intercourse with the interior, and . . . afford, at no distant day, an inland communication from the Atlantic States to Louisiana. . . ."[8] A man of prominence "intimated the idea of an interior communication from Darien, in Georgia, to New Orleans, as a thing very easy to accomplish. . . ."[9]

The subject was discussed in Washington as well as on the frontier. Calhoun, Secretary of War, reported to Congress that "It only remains to consider the system of roads and canals connected with the defense of our Southern frontier, or that on the Gulf of Mexico. . . . The continuation of the road along the Atlantic coast from Milledgeville to New Orleans. . . ."[10] President James Monroe was also interested in the movement of people. Thomas Jefferson in a communication to Albert Gallatin wrote that "emigration to the West and South is going on beyond anything imaginable. The President told me lately that the sales of public land would amount to ten millions of dollars."[11]

How did the people get into the South? Over what roads did they travel? What was the condition of the roads? These are a few of the questions that must be answered in order to have an adequate idea of travel in the South.

Savannah was founded in 1733, and in 1735 a road was

[8] *Niles' Weekly Register*, XVI (1819), 44.
[9] *Ibid.*
[10] *American State Papers, Miscellaneous*, II, 535.
[11] *The Writings of Albert Gallatin*, II, 89.

designed leading into the West; which road seems to have been the first authorized by the Colonial Assembly. The record made at that time stated that "there are forty men appointed to clear a path from Barnwell's Bluff (north side of Alletamaha River—south settlement) to Savannah, and Mr Oglethorpe design's, that every six miles shall be a village, and that at every River there shall be another with a Ferry Boat."[12]

These early roads were through new country, many of them being hastily constructed without proper drainage; therefore the rains "rendered the roads almost impassable, and the streams so swollen that fording them has become dangerous to travellers."[13]

During the year 1736 three townships were settled, Frederica, Darien, and Augusta,[14] which needed to be connected with Savannah by roads. Numerous references are found in the records of the colony of Georgia, sometimes the mention of a name, other times a description of a road.[15] The small villages, poor roads, and frontier conditions made Georgia appear an undesirable place. Reverend George Whitefield arrived in Savannah on the 10th of January, 1739/40, and seemed to have been favorably impressed, for he wrote to Newman that "Savannah is not so bad a state as is represented abroad."[16] "As poor as a Georgian"[17] became a proverbial expression that indicated the unfavorable conditions existing in a frontier settlement, deprived of the advantages of the markets of the longer established communities, deprived of the stabilizing effect of a larger population, and deprived of the communication afforded by good roads. This was not an uncommon condition in an

---
[12] *Colonial Records of Georgia*, XXI, 115.
[13] *Ibid.*, pp. 294, 470.   [14] *Ibid.*, p. 414.
[15] *Ibid.*, IV, 127; XXII (pt. II), 28, 215, 238, 351; XXII (pt. I), 59, 120, 262.
[16] *Ibid.*, XXII (pt. II), 300.   [17] *Ibid.*, p. 394.

outpost settlement, for until a colony was well established, good roads were impossible. There was always the problem of defraying expenses. Should the trustees bear the expense, or should the people have a share in building and maintaining the road? A letter concerning the question of roads stated that

it is certain, Sir, that good roads are of the greatest benefit to any country, and those two represented as necessary to be done by the assembly, wou'd doubtless be of unknown service to this, but we think, if they mean the trustees to make them wholly, that they have asked a favour, which must create a monstrous expense. If indeed their honours shou'd be pleased to be at the expense of Ferry-boats to cross certain Rivers, or if making bridges over some creeks, we think it wou'd be highly reasonable, that the inhabitants should be obliged by law made for that purpose to make roads, as in other colonys.[18]

This general condition prevailed until 1755 when an act was passed "to empower the several surveyors hereafter named to lay out Public Roads in the Province of Georgia."[19] The surveyors named in the act were authorized to lay out such high roads, private paths, bridges, causeways, and to establish such ferries as they thought proper.[20]

The duties were—

1. To assess towns, etc., for repair work on roads, in case the work could not be done by the surveyor.[21]
2. To make contracts for the building of bridges, and to levy on all male inhabitants, money or labor, to carry it out.[22]
3. To appoint someone in the district to summon all persons to work.[23]

[18] Ibid., XXVI, 167, 168.
[19] Ibid., XVIII, 88.
[20] Ibid.
[21] Ibid., p. 92.
[22] Ibid., p. 93.
[23] Ibid.

4. To appoint one or more overseers to attend, view, direct, and manage the work going on.[24]
5. To meet at least twice a year.
    a. Easter Monday.
    b. First Monday in August.
        (1) To divide the roads, paths, etc., among the surveyors for special attention.
        (2) To assign every person liable for work.
        (3) To choose another surveyor in case one had left, died, or was incapable.[25]
6. To be accountable to the Governor and Council, or the General Assembly when sitting.[26]
7. To subdivide districts.[27]
8. To be bound when on the road by the orders of one as they would be by the orders of all.[28]
9. To establish ferries where they deemed it necessary, to procure proper boats and persons to attend them, and to settle the scale of fares.[29]
10. To have the authority to call for work on cut offs on the creeks or rivers, the persons so employed being exempt from their road work.[30]
11. To lay out any roads or paths that were needed by the people.[31]
12. To enforce the limit of work for which anyone was liable.
    a. Not more than 6 days at a time.
    b. Not more than 2 times in one year.[32]

The specifications for the roads established and authorized by this act were; (1) Each road should be 24 feet wide, (2) Trees should be left near the line of the road for shade.[33]

[24] *Ibid.*, p. 95.
[25] *Ibid.*, XVIII, 98.
[26] *Ibid.*, p. 99.
[27] *Ibid.*
[28] *Ibid.*
[29] *Ibid.*, p. 100.
[30] *Ibid.*
[31] *Ibid.*, XVIII, 100, 101.
[32] *Ibid.*, p. 101.
[33] *Ibid.*, p. 96.

The act also drew up a schedule of fines. The crimes punishable were numerous as the list of fines shows:

1. 2 shillings sterling per diam.. Anyone who refused to pay money or find labor for repairs of road.[34]
2. 30 shillings .... for not summoning people for work.[35]
3. 2 shillings per diam per person .... for each person not going to work that was under him.[36]
4. not exceeding 2 shillings per diam .... for first fault on road work.[37]
5. not exceeding 2 shillings plus 20 shillings.......... for continued fault on road work.[38]
6. 30 shillings .... for overseer refusing to do his duty.[39]
7. not exceeding £5 .... for refusing to clear road, etc., of material that he was responsible for having there.[40]
8. 20 shillings .... for cutting down trees within 10 feet of road.[41]
9. 20 shillings .... for every offense of surveyor in neglect of duty.[42]
10. £5 .... for every offense of any person that hindered the surveyor from making or mending the road.[43]

The roads of southeastern Georgia were built under these provisions, which proving inadequate were amended in 1757 to cover certain specifications, as follows—

[34] *Ibid.*, p. 92.
[35] *Ibid.*, p. 94.
[36] *Ibid.*
[37] *Ibid.*, XVIII, 95.
[38] *Ibid.*
[39] *Ibid.*
[40] *Ibid.*, p. 96.
[41] *Ibid.*, p. 97.
[42] *Ibid.*
[43] *Ibid.*

1. ½ male inhabitants of Savannah, between the ages of 16 and 60, should clear and keep the town and commons of Savannah free from woods, bushes, trees, etc.[44]
2. the other ½ should work on the Southwest Road.[45]
3. ¼ part of all fines should be used for the Public Wharf at Savannah.[46]
4. no fees for landing to be paid by the inhabitants of the province except when they remained over 24 hours.[47]

With this organization and with the territory divided into districts, each supervised by five to seven surveyors, road construction was carried on. The districts designated were:

Town Division
1st Northwest Division
2nd Northwest Division
3rd Northwest Division
Upper Old Road, Fording Place on the Beaver dam up to McBean's swamp
4th Northwest Division
The Newington Road
1st Southwest Division
2nd Southwest Division
3rd Southwest Division
4th Southwest Division
Land lying between the Altamaha and St. Mary Rivers
Eastern Division
Southern Division.[48]

Although there was systematic organization, the plan when put into operation was not successful. The records of travel through Georgia are filled with references to the poor

[44] *Ibid.*, XVIII, 183.
[45] *Ibid.*
[46] *Ibid.*, p. 184.
[47] *Ibid.*
[48] *Ibid.*, XXIII, 719-28.

condition of the roads, ferries, and bridges. Travel was difficult outside the thickly settled area, the roads many times being absolutely impassable. One record, dated 1757, noted that "many of his Majesty's subjects settled on the Southern Frontier of this Province who are obliged to attend in Assembly and at the General Court at Savannah are put to great inconveniencys for want of a road to open a communication from the town of Savannah to Great Ogeechee."[49]

Another traveler a few years later observed that

the roads are good or bad according to the difference of the ground. In a sandy soil the roads are dry and good; but in a clayey one they are bad. The people here are likewise very careless in mending them. If a rivulet be not very great they do not make a bridge over it; and travellers may do as well as they can to get over: therefore many people are in danger of being drowned in such places, where the water is risen by a heavy rain. When a tree falls across the road, it is seldom cut off, to keep the road clear, but the people go around it. This they can easily do, since the ground is very even, and without stones; has no under-wood or shrubs, and the trees on it stand much asunder. Hence the roads here have so many bendings.[50]

Roads radiated from Savannah in every direction. One road was constructed northward toward Augusta; another went southward toward Florida connecting intermediate points. Then there was the western road that led to New Orleans. In most instances they were the same paths that had previously been used by the traders, but were widened so as to accommodate a wagon and later, the stage-coach. The construction did not vary to any great extent and could hardly be called improved, since many times stumps of trees were left in the road to be dodged by the driver, if he could

[49] *Ibid.*, XVIII, 182.
[50] Peter Kolm, *Travels into North America*, I, 24, 25.

do so. It was not an uncommon sight to see a wagon delayed with a broken wheel, but the immigrant was not particularly distressed by such an occurrence. He had plenty of time, for he desired only to arrive at his destination before bad weather. He generally carried enough provisions for the first year as he could not build his house and make a crop too.

Augusta, situated on the Savannah River just below the falls, also played a major part in the development of transportation facilities in Georgia.

The trustees ordered the town of Augusta to be laid off in 1735, and garrisoned in 1736, several warehouses were built and furnished with goods suitable for the Indian trade—boats were built by the inhabitants calculated to carry about ten thousand weight of peltry; making four or five voyages annually to Charleston. Augusta became a general resort for the Indian traders in the spring, where they purchased annually about two thousand pack-horse loads of peltry: and including towns-men, pack-horse-men and servants, it was calculated that six hundred white persons were engaged in this trade.[51]

The value of Augusta as a trading center was obvious. Therefore a road or path was marked out through the woods to Savannah to supplement the river as a means of communication.[52]

From Augusta three paths led into the Indian country: the Upper Trading Path, the Middle Trading Path, and the Lower Trading Path. The Upper led through the Cherokee country and the territory claimed by Tennessee. The other two passed through the Upper and Lower Creek Nations and were the ones more generally used in travelling to the Southwest. The Middle Path followed the fall line and was more important than the Lower, which led into the "forked country" between the Chattahoochee and the Flint Rivers.

[51] Hugh M'Call, *History of Georgia*, I, 34, 55.
[52] MacGill, *op. cit.*, p. 252.

"The road from Savannah to Augusta is, for the most part, through Pine barrens; but more uneven than I had been accustomed to since leavg. Petersburg in Virginia."[53] This statement was made by George Washington following his tour in 1791. He continued by saying, "The roads are abominably sandy and heavy—my horses (especially the two I bought just before I left Philadelphia, and my old white horse) are much worn down and I have yet 150 or 200 miles of heavy sand to pass before I fairly get into the upper and firmer roads."[54]

Judge Walton, in a speech to a grand jury in Wilkes County in 1785, made an interesting statement: ". . . I look forward to a time, not far distant, when . . . the whole [of Georgia] will be settled and connected . . . from the shore of the Atlantic to the banks of the Mississippi."[55] This represents the trend of thought of those on the Atlantic coast and it gave impetus to those that were developing the means of transportation. Men with a far-sighted vision were the prophets of the new age in modes of travel. And this new age was ushered in, not so much by the trader, important though he was, as by the United States post office service, with its many mail-coaches and still greater number of post-riders plying over regular, established routes. This department of the government aided in improving and maintaining the roads.

[53] George Washington, *The Diaries of George Washington*, IV, 179.
[54] *Letters and Recollections of George Washington*, p. 40.
[55] Whitaker, *op. cit.*, p. 6, quoted from *Gazette of the State of Georgia*, April 14, 1785.

CHAPTER IV
THE DEVELOPMENT OF POST ROADS

WELL ORGANIZED post roads were unknown in the South before the year 1803, which was a pivotal year in the history of western expansion. On December 20, 1803, the United States received from France the southern section of Louisiana, the transfer taking place in New Orleans according to the terms of the "Purchase" that had been agreed upon. Then, as never before, there was intense interest in communication with New Orleans, the capital of the newly acquired territory. Discussion of the need was equally important to two groups: first, those living in western Georgia; and second, those residing in the "crescent city" on the Mississippi River. It has been said of the earlier period that "the postal service did more than any one other agency to unify and unite the colonists. It brought their interests and endeavours to a common meeting point."[1] This was equally true of the opening years of the nineteenth century.

The absolute necessity of a connecting link between the seaboard and the Mississippi Valley was apparent. For unity New Orleans had to be made immediately accessible, a condition that did not exist at that time. It was separated from the East by miles of trackless forests. It was necessary to have mail move more rapidly between the far-removed city and Washington.

The route, in order to be of the most service, must be as short as the nature of the country would permit. "On November 2, 1803, before the transfer of New Orleans was accomplished, Samuel L. Mitchell had introduced in the

[1] Washington, D. C., *Evening Star*, July 26, 1913, quoted in Louis Melius, *The American Postal Service*, p. 17.

DEVELOPMENT OF POST ROADS

House of Representatives a resolution providing 'that the committee on Post Offices and Post Roads be directed to inquire by what means the mail may be conveyed with greater facility and dispatch, than at present, between the city of Washington and Natchez and New Orleans.' "[2] This was adopted without division.

There was at this time a long and circuitous route between Washington and New Orleans, a route which extended to "Knoxville and Nashville, in Tennessee, and from thence, through the wilderness, by Natchez, to New Orleans —a distance of more than fifteen hundred miles."[3] The suggestion was made and later communicated to the House of Representatives that a road be laid out and improved in as direct a line between Washington and New Orleans as the mountains would permit. The Appalachian Mountains formed a barrier that had to be conquered before direct east and west communication could be established. The passes through the mountain range had been utilized by the trader in establishing the earlier routes to the Southwest, trails that were long and tiring and beset with many hazards. The proposed route, to be used by the mail carrier, extended through the Atlantic states until the foothills of the mountains were reached in Georgia. From there the route followed the fall line through the Indian country to New Orleans, the ultimate destination.

Postmaster General Gideon Granger, in answer to a question of James Jackson, chairman of the Committee of the Senate investigating the post roads, said that "many embarrassments and difficulties will present themselves in passing the mountains, and completing the establishments in the Western States."[4]

David Thomas of the Committee on Post Offices and

[2] *Annals of Congress,* 8th Congress, 1st Session, I, 555.
[3] *American State Papers, Post Office,* p. 28.
[4] *Ibid.,* p. 29.

Post Roads in a report concerning the feasibility of the proposed road around the southern end of the Appalachian Mountains said

that by establishing a post route, as nigh, on a direct line between those two cities, as the Blue Ridge and Alleghany Mountains will admit of, will not only lessen the distance about five hundred miles, but, as this will pass almost the whole way through a country inhabited either by citizens of the United States, or friendly Indians, the mail will be more secure. . . .[5]

One month later, January 12, 1804, the committee had changed its opinion. The proposed route would have to pass through the Mississippi Territory for a distance of nearly four hundred miles, wholly uninhabited by citizens of the United States, except on the Tombigbee River. The committee concluded that until this country could be explored it was not in their power to designate the proper route with any degree of precision. Therefore a resolution was adopted, specifying "that the mail ought to be carried on the present route, as established by law, from the city of Washington to Knoxville, in Tennessee, . . . from thence by Tellico Block House, and through the Cherokee nation of Indians, and the settlement on the Tombigbee river, to New Orleans."[6]

The southern route was interesting, but existing conditions must be taken into consideration. First, the route would have to be surveyed, as mentioned in David Thomas' report, and definitely located; second, permission would have to be secured from the Indians to cut the road through their Nation. Thomas Jefferson, President of the United States, in discussing this plan with Isaac Briggs, a government surveyor who, within a short time, was leaving Washington for the Southwest, impressed upon him how anxious he was to have "a direct road from Washington to New Or-

[5] *Ibid.*, p. 28.   [6] *Ibid.*, p. 30.

DEVELOPMENT OF POST ROADS

leans, which should not cross the mountains at all."[7] Briggs was interested in the undertaking and offered to follow the proposed line on his expedition to Natchez. Jefferson commissioned him to make the survey, and in a communication to the House stated the conditions under which Briggs undertook the commission:

Isaac Briggs, one of the surveyors general of the United States, being about to return in July last to his station at Natchez, and apprised of the anxiety existing to have a practicable road explored for forwarding the mail to New Orleans, without crossing the mountains, offered his services voluntarily to return by the route contemplated, taking, as he should go, such observations of longitude and latitude as should enable him to delineate it exactly, and, by protraction, to show of what shortening it would admit. The offer was accepted, and he was furnished with an accurate sextant for his observations. The route proposed was from Washington, by Fredericksburg, Cartersville, Lower Sauratown, Salisbury, Franklin Court House, in Georgia, Tuckaubatchee, Fort Stoddert, and the mouth of Pearl river, to New Orleans.[8]

Briggs proceeded on his way to New Orleans over a route that was not altogether definite, and one which, although it seemed favourable when laid out on a map, was yet to become an actuality. His duty was to travel over the route, to plot it, making the necessary observations, and then to submit a detailed report to the President. He wrote several letters to President Jefferson while on the trip, giving a graphic picture of the hardships he was undergoing.

In the first letter which came from Clarksborough, Georgia, dated September 2, 1804, he said that

Attending to the necessary observations, under the frequent in-

[7] *Ibid., Claims,* p. 362.
[8] *Ibid., Post Office,* p. 35; also cf. correspondence of Briggs in the *Jefferson Papers* (Library of Congress) and the *Letterbook of Isaac Briggs* (Library of Congress).

terruptions of clouds, keeping a regular series of notes, and the rest absolutely requisite to repair the fatigues of travelling in weather so extremely hot as we have had it, have prevented us from making a more rapid progress on our journey, and have compelled me to be a much less attentive correspondent than I expected, or intended to have been . . . in order to obtain some important information from General Meriwether respecting our route, we are here about twenty miles to the left of our course.

In consequence of the labor of making astronomical observations, and of the hot weather, I have found this, I think, both to body and mind, the most fatiguing journey I ever undertook.[9]

One month later another letter out of the wilderness came to Jefferson from Briggs, who wrote from Colonel Hawkins' establishment in Georgia. The tone of both communications was the same—a whole-hearted endeavor to overcome the impossible. The letter disclosed that an assistant was necessary to make the observations that were required, and Thomas Robertson was secured to act in that capacity. Briggs continued his letter by saying that they proceeded from Clarksborough to General Meriwether's for the much needed information. They were furnished in addition to the information, a pack horse and provisions for their journey as far as Colonel Hawkins', on the Flint River. The preparation necessarily delayed them for several days. A more vivid picture may be had from an excerpt from the letter:

On the 6th we departed from General Meriwether's, and after wandering many miles astray in the wilderness, we arrived on the 8th at the store of an Indian trader, about thirty-one miles from General Meriwether's. Here we were delayed two days by severe and stormy weather; sometimes the ear could scarcely distinguish an interval between the sound of one falling tree and that of another. Having made many fruitless efforts to procure a guide to Colonel Hawkins's, (a distance of about sixty miles) we travelled or rather wandered at least one hundred and twelve

[9] *American State Papers, Post Office*, p. 36.

miles, frequently climbing over precipices, wandering through swamps, and crossing the deep and difficult water courses, many miles without a path, our horses greatly incommoded and fatigued by sensitive briers and other vines. Our provisions were soon wet and spoiled, and we were in danger of starving, not having seen a human face except each other's, for more than four days; on the 15th we arrived at Colonel Hawkins's, on Flint river.

From Colonel Hawkins we received the most polite and friendly treatment, and every assistance in his power. He informed us that, had we made the attempt sooner in the season, it would have been impossible for us to have passed through, for the scarcity of provisions had been such that the nation has been almost in a state of famine—and that the large horse flies would have destroyed our horses; having actually killed many.

The Colonel having furnished us with a packhorse, provisions, and a guide, on the 20th we proceeded, and on the 27th we arrived here, (one hundred and twenty miles) after a journey the most laborious, both to ourselves and our horses. There having fallen a very heavy rain after we left Flint river, we found the rivers, creeks, and low ground, so full of water, so rapid, and so entangled with vines, as to threaten almost a certainty of drowning our horses, if not ourselves, should we attempt to cross before the waters had subsided, so that we could see by the bushes the course of the path. Our horses swam the Chattahoochee river from shore to shore, and six creeks between that and this place. In short, we arrived here much fatigued.

I had an idea that I could pass through this country without a path or a guide, but when I mentioned it on the frontiers of Georgia, it was scouted and laughed at, and I am now firmly of opinion that, in this way, it would be at least a *four months'* passage from Georgia to New Orleans. I have at this place seen two of the principal chiefs of the nations, Oche Hajo, and Esau Hajo; they appear to be very friendly, and well disposed toward the United States. . . .

P. S. 3rd, in the morning, we are just about to mount our horses, and expect to be at Fort Stoddert in six or seven days.[10]

[10] *Ibid.*, pp. 35, 36.

The next letter from Briggs was not written until the 26th of November, and by that time he had reached his goal, New Orleans. That letter follows:

I wrote to thee on the 2d of the 10th month, from the south easternmost projection of Tallapoosa river, which I call Point Comfort. Next morning (3d) we left Point Comfort, and proceeding on the southeast side of Alabama river, nearly parallel with its course, we arrived, on the 9th, at the house of Nathaniel Christmas, on the west side of the Tombigbee river, about two miles above its confluence with Alabama. At this place I received certain intelligence that the yellow fever at this time raged in New Orleans with uncommon violence, and was peculiarly fatal to visitants from other places: so that I deemed it prudent to delay my entrance into that city until a change in the weather, and future intelligence, should offer me some prospect of safety. I had also, on the very day of my arrival here, another visit from my old acquaintance the autumnal intermittent fever. For these reasons I remained on Tombigbee three weeks, industriously employing all the time my indisposition allowed me, in calculating the geographical position of places on my route. Although my arrival in New Orleans has been several weeks later, my report on the post road will not be one day delayed by my remaining on Tombigbee.

On the 29th ultimo we left Tombigbee, passing through the town of Mobile; we crossed Pascagoula river near its mouth, passed round the bays of Biloxi and St. Louis, to Pearl river, about ten miles above its mouth. From thence we passed down Pearl river, through the rigolets and lake to New Orleans. On this part of our route, (a distance of about two hundred miles) we were twenty-five days. To give some idea of the difficulties we have encountered, besides the insurmountable delays of transporting our horses over rivers several miles wide, where there are no ferries, I will mention the progress we made in one fatiguing, industrious, and laborious day's travelling, when, entangled among impassable and boggy drains, which are very frequent, and of considerable length, we encamped at night about three miles from our encampment on the preceding night. Yet these obstacles might be easily overcome by a little labor, and a road, in my opinion, may be made on the route which we have contemplated, with much less expense, and far superior to the best gravelled turnpike in the Middle States. The practicable distance from the city of Washington to this place, will be very little more than one thousand miles.[11]

The major communication from Briggs took the form of a report, dated December 22, 1804. It was written in New Orleans and was communicated to the House of Representatives on February 23, 1805, by President Jefferson.[12]

The first part of the report was devoted to a discussion of the difficulties of obtaining celestial observations. The weather had been so inclement during the entire trip and portions of the terrain so impassable, that the journey consumed more time than had been originally anticipated. The road as recommended in this report would connect certain major points, the exact locations of the local roads that would join these cities to be determined later. The general direction and nature of the country was all that was expected of Briggs. A more detailed survey under the authority of the Post Office Department would follow and supplement this preliminary view.

The cities listed in the report were:

Fredericksburg ⎫
Cartersville   ⎬ In Virginia
Danville   ⎭
Salisbury, in North Carolina
Athens, in Georgia
Point Comfort, southeasternmost projection of Tallapoosa river, (Creek Nation)
Mobile River, just below the confluence of the Allabama and Tombigbee
New Orleans[13]

[11] *Ibid.*, p. 36.   [12] *Ibid.*   [13] *Ibid.*, p. 37.

The bearings and distances in British statute miles, of these major points along the route were next given in the report.

From Washington, New Orleans	bears	S	54°	13'	47"	W	
							965.0
" New Orleans, Washington	"	N	46	48	15	E	
" Washington, Fredericksburg	"	S	19	22	29	W	
							49.1
" Fredericksburg, Washington	"	N	19	11	28	E	
" Fredericksburg, Salisbury	"	S	50	39	17	W	
							268.6
" Salisbury, Fredericksburg	"	N	48	26	4	E	
" Salisbury, Franklin Court House	"	S	58	41	12	W	
							179.6
" Franklin Court House, Salisbury	"	N	57	10	7	E	
" Franklin Court House, Point Comfort	"	S	46	54	30	W	
							196.2
" Point Comfort, Franklin Court House	"	N	45	33	26	E	
" Point Comfort, Mouth of Allabama River	"	S	52	39	39	W	
							143.4
" Mouth of Alabama River, Point Comfort	"	N	51	38	51	E	
" Mouth of Alabama River, New Orleans	"	S	56	31	47	W	
							142.6
" New Orleans, Mouth of Alabama River	"	N	55	31	12	E	

Whole distance 979.5[14]

[14] *Ibid.*

DEVELOPMENT OF POST ROADS

The latitudes and longtitudes ascertained by observations were also given in the report, the President's House being used as the zero of longitude.

	Latitude	Longitude
Washington	38° 53′ 00″	00° 00′ 00″
Fredericksburg	38 12 43	0 18 00
Salisbury	35 41 43	4 00 00
Franklin Court House	34 21 12	6 41 20
Clarksborough	33 57 30	0 00 00
Hawkins's on Flint River	32 39 00	7 25 11
Point Comfort, on Tallapoosa	32 23 19	9 8 38
Mouth of Alabama	31 6 57	11 4 48
New Orleans	29 57 45	13 3 30[15]

The concluding paragraphs of the report were devoted to a detailed description of the route in order to familiarize the President with the country. The general character of the soil, the streams that crossed the proposed route, the possibility of improving the condition of these crossings, and the need of further surveys were all dealt with in the report.

In Louisiana at this time, 1803-1804, there was also interest in road building, as was shown in the laws of the territory. One section stated that

the keeping in repair of bridges, roads, and mounds being indispensable for the facility of transportation, for the convenience of the inhabitants and travellers, and for the preservation of the fruits of the earth, the syndics shall direct their whole attention to that object with an impartiality and firmness proof against all reproach and worldly considerations.[16]

Steps were being taken to connect isolated sections of Louisiana. A post road was opened between Loftus Heights and

[15] *Ibid.*
[16] Digest of Laws of Louisiana submitted to Congress, *American State Papers, Miscellaneous*, I, 379.

New Orleans;[17] an office was established in Baton Rouge[18] to handle the mail; and there was being discussed the possibility of opening a road through Florida that would link with New Orleans.[19] Governor Claiborne was eager to connect the Louisiana roads with the road to the East. In a letter to the Postmaster General the Governor outlined the best approach to his city,[20] which was by way of Bayou Catherine. He added that if this way was not desirable, a road could be opened up without great difficulty. It would be necessary to throw up small levees in some places, as the high winds from the southeast occasionally forced the water of the Gulf of Mexico over the banks at particular places. In southern Mississippi and Louisiana the waterways were continuously a problem; the best way to solve the problem would be to use them rather than attempt to build a road that would necessarily have to cross them.

Isaac Briggs, after making the difficult journey from the Georgia frontier to New Orleans in behalf of the public, did not receive his compensation. The survey was made in 1804, and in 1808 he was still trying to get some recompense for it. In a letter dated May 25, 1807, from Thomas Jefferson, addressed to Briggs, we can ascertain the stand he took on the question.

Dear Sir,

When you spoke to me the other day on the subject of your expenses to New Orleans, my answer was a little indefinite as to time, because I had just received some very heavy bills drawn on me from Europe, and I had not yet examined what would be the state of my funds under those bills. I have now examined them, and find that I can furnish you two hundred dollars on the 6th of June, . . . and $200 dollars more on that day month, if this will answer your purposes. I am really mortified that

[17] *Official Letter Books of W. C. C. Claiborne*, II, 206.
[18] *Ibid.*, pp. 212, 213.
[19] *Ibid.*, III, 37, 38.   [20] *Ibid.*, pp. 97, 98.

you should have been left to suffer in an undertaking wherein I was an agent; but you know with what expectations we concluded on it. My own opinion has always been, that, where a person undertakes to do a thing for the public, unauthorized by law, he does it justly on his own risk, and that the public are perfectly free to approve or reject. In this case, Congress have fully approved by building on the foundations you laid. We are now establishing our road on your survey, availing ourselves of it solely as having saved us the necessity of making any other. Gentlemen who say they will never sanction an expenditure made without a previous law, will leave their country exposed to incalculable injury in those unforeseen occurrences where the voluntary sacrifices of virtuous citizens might save the public interest. . . .[21]

About ten months later Briggs presented a petition to the House of Representatives in which he said that "your petitioner, . . . relying on your mercy and liberality, prays that you allow him such compensation as you may deem just and reasonable."[22] Whether his petition was granted or not is uncertain; it appears that the funds received from President Jefferson were his only compensation.[23]

In the laying out of post roads between Washington and New Orleans, the relationship between the United States government and the Indians was complicated and important, and treaties had to be promulgated, securing permission from the Indians to run roads through their lands and, as far as possible, arranging for the safe transportation of the mail. For example, it had been decided that the mail be transported from Knoxville to New Orleans through Indian country. The agents of the United States and those of the Cherokees met at Tellico and drew up a treaty which was signed October 27, 1805. It stipulated that

[21] *American State Papers, Claims*, p. 362.
[22] *Ibid.*
[23] MacGill, *op. cit.*, p. 58 n.

Whereas the mail of the United States is ordered to be carried from Knoxville to New Orleans through Cherokee, Creek, and Choctaw countries; the Cherokees agree that the citizens of the United States shall have, so far as it goes through their country, the free and unmolested use of a road leading from Tellico to Tombigbe, to be laid out by viewers appointed by both sides, who shall direct it the nearest and best way....[24]

In the following year further arrangements were made to continue the road, this time with the Creek Indians. The opening of the road had to be sanctioned by each group through whose territory it passed in order that the mail might be carried safely. On November 14, 1805, the negotiators met in Washington and signed the treaty which stated that it had been "agreed, on the part of the Creek nation that the Government of the United States shall forever hereafter have a right to a horse path, through the Creek country, from the Ocmulgee to the Mobile, in such direction as shall . . . be considered most convenient, and to clear out the same, and lay logs over the creeks."[25]

With arrangements such as these it would seem that peaceful relations would exist, but the contrary was true in every locality. The press of the period was filled with accounts of banditry and murder. Benjamin Hawkins, agent for Indian Affairs, in a letter to Colonel Nicolls, commander of His Majesty's forces stationed at Apalachicola, discussed this condition and asked support and assistance in overcoming the situation. ". . . one man was killed and four wounded on the post road. Our waggons twice attacked and one waggoner killed several horses taken and carried, as reported, to your depot, at the very time the waggons were carrying seed corn for the Indians, and flour for the support

[24] *Indian Affairs, Laws and Treaties*, II, 84; *American State Papers, Indian Affairs*, I, 698; 7 Stat. 96.
[25] *Indian Affairs, Laws and Treaties*, II, 85; 7 Stat. 96.

of nearly 5,000 totally destitute of food."²⁶ Such circumstances might have been relieved, according to a report from the Chickasaw agency, by sending a company of regular soldiers to a point where friction was likely to occur. In times of trouble they would be of inestimable value, and in times of peace they "would be employed in making improvements on the road, and in removing and keeping intruders from off the Indian land."²⁷

Many other treaties were made with the Indians governing specific points and were of varying importance; some concerning ferries, ferry houses, and tolls, others dealing with houses of accommodation. These houses were dignified by the titles of "Inn" and "Tavern," but they were miserable hovels as is attested in every travel account of the period. The Indians, under treaty arrangements, were to maintain houses of entertainment, to be located advantageously along the road. The treaties stipulated the charges to be made but did not necessarily mention the services to be rendered.

These treaties remained in force, at least theoretically, until others were made whereby the Indians relinquished their rights to the land in the Southern states and agreed to remove to the Indian Territory west of the Mississippi. With the removal of the Indians the roads could be made without the handicap of traversing Indian territory.

In the meantime, however, trouble with the Indians did not check the road building activity of the United States government. On February 4, 1807, the legislature approved an act to appoint "commissioners to view, mark, and open a good road on the nearest route from the city of Natchez to Fort Stoddert so as to intersect the new Creek road from Knoxville on the line of demarcation east of the Pearl

[26] *Niles' Weekly Register*, VIII (1815), 287; cf. X (1816), 231; XI (1816-17), 63.
[27] *American State Papers, Indian Affairs*, II, 80.

River."[28] The following summer Harry Toulmir, James Coller, and Lemuel Henry were appointed commissioners to carry out the instructions of the legislature. On the 7th of December the following notice was given to the public; that "the ferry is now complete over the Alabama River, above Little River, and on the Tombigbee, just above Fort St. Stephens."[29] The road was then open and marked with causeways across all branches and boggy places. According to John W. Monette[30] it was the first road opened from the western to the eastern part of the Territory. Over it a traveler could pass with safety, by observing the three notches, or "three-chopped way."[31] The name, "three-chopped way," originated early in the history of the road. The surveyors as they went through the country laying out the route marked it with the "triple blaze," and it is from this method of marking the trail that the road derives its name. This road made the distance shorter between Natchez and Georgia.[32]

While the road development was taking place in Louisiana, Albert Gallatin was formulating a report which he submitted to the Senate on April 4, 1808, in which he outlined the need of governmental aid in the building of a road through the wilderness.

The portions of road which, traversing a wilderness cannot be improved without the aid of the United States, are, from ... Nashville in Tennessee, or Athens in Georgia, to Natchez. The expense necessary to enable the mail and even stages to proceed at the rate of about two hundred miles, including bridges over the small streams, be estimated, for those ... roads, at two hundred thousand dollars.[33]

[28] Dunbar Rowland, *History of Mississippi*, II, 568.
[29] *Ibid.*
[30] John W. Monette, *History of the Discovery and Settlement of the Valley of the Mississippi*, II, 380.
[31] Peter A. Brannon, "Three Notch Road," *Arrow Points*, VII (1923), 35-38.
[32] The distance from Natchez to Milledgeville over this road was 545 miles. For a table of distances on this road, see Rowland, *op. cit.*, p. 569.
[33] *American State Papers, Miscellaneous*, I, 739.

DEVELOPMENT OF POST ROADS   65

Two years later the route was well established, as was attested by a communication addressed to Stephen F. Austin from Isaac L. Baker. Baker was at Transylvania University when he wrote the letter, which was dated July 1, 1810. He was considering a trip to Texas by way of New Orleans. Our interests are centered on the first stage of the trip, concerning which he commented: "if no passage can be had or the road from St. Genevieve to Chickasaw Bluffs is impracticable at that season I will go via Knoxville, Savannah, and Mobile for the old beaten track I have seen often enough. . . ."[34] Many more people might have traveled this new route had it been considered safe. However, brigands infested it, mails were delayed if not robbed while in transit,[35] and the trip was so hazardous that some travelers chose the longer but safer water route, to New Orleans. Other accounts of misfortune along the roads are told by Otto Rothert in his book entitled, *Outlaws of Cave-in-Rock*. The traveler was kept in constant fear of his own safety and the safety of those with him.

In January, 1812, a notice was published stating that "the road from Fort Hawkins to Fort Stoddart through the Indian territory is complete. . . ."[36] Eight years had elapsed since Isaac Briggs, surveyor of the lands of the United States south of the State of Tennessee, made his difficult and little appreciated trip through this wilderness. Later years showed that he was the pioneer and others, as they came along accepted, completed, and popularized his route through southern Alabama and Mississippi connecting the frontier of Georgia with New Orleans.[37]

At that time the usual rate of travel in the transportation

[34] "Austin Papers," ed. by Eugene C. Barker, *American Historical Association Annual Report*, 1919, II (pt. I), 175.
[35] *Official Letter Books of W. C. C. Claiborne*, V, 94; VI, 103.
[36] *Niles' Weekly Register*, I (1811-12), 376.
[37] Adam Seybert, *Annales Statistiques des États-Unis*, p. 241.

of mail in the Central States was forty miles per day on cross roads and in making less important connections. The majority of the routes in the South were not improved but were similar to the cross roads farther north; therefore, forty miles per day would be a fair estimate of the speed that could be maintained. It may be added as a basis of comparison, that between the larger northern commercial towns the distance covered per day was increased to sixty miles, and when the occasion arose it was possible to cover one hundred and twenty miles in twenty-four hours. Furthermore on such well constructed routes as those radiating from Philadelphia to New York, Baltimore, and Washington the speed was increased still more to the average of seven miles per hour.[38] Forty miles or even sixty miles a day was very slow movement for mail when one considers the great distances that had to be covered. This speed was of course dependent upon good roads. The question of keeping the post road in repair was an important topic and merited much consideration. In 1815 a report was submitted to the House of Representatives by the Committee on Post Roads, which discussed and made recommendations "on the expediency of repairing and keeping in repair" the roads from Nashville to Natchez and Fort Hawkins to St. Stephens.[39] It was necessary to keep the undergrowth cut down and renew the causeways and bridges after spring freshets, entailing a great amount of work, but it could not be ignored if the mails were to go through.

This was the period of the War of 1812, and as a result of the slowness of communication, hostilities were continued long after the treaty of peace had been signed. In Ghent, on December 24, 1814, the treaty was signed and theoretically the war was over; but in New Orleans, far removed as it

[38] MacGill, *op. cit.*, p. 58.
[39] *American State Papers, Miscellaneous*, II, 273.

was, no one knew of the peace, and on January 8, 1815, the Battle of New Orleans was fought.

On February 14, 1815, R. J. Meigs, Postmaster General, addressed a communication to the postmasters, contractors, and others on the route from Washington City to New Orleans. This letter constitutes a valuable commentary on the post roads and general conditions with regard to movement of mail in the South:

> Sir—Mr. Charles Bell, the bearer hereof, is charged with dispatches relative to the state of peace which has taken place between the United States and Great Britain. I need not mention to you the importance of forwarding these dispatches with the greatest expedition possible, and have only to request your aid in furnishing or procuring horses, or in case Mr. Bell should be unable to proceed, to employ a new messenger, so often as occasion may require, to forward these dispatches· to New Orleans; any necessary expence which may be incurred in this respect, shall be duly reimbursed from this office.
>
> R. J. Meigs
> Post Master General

> Mr. Bell will rest four hours at night, and travel 80 miles in day-time, and proceed as far as he can stand it. The rider may take the lower road direct to Columbia, so as to pass on the shortest route.[40]

The *Niles' Weekly Register* made an interesting comment on this trip of Charles Bell:

> The dispatch bearer of the above ratified treaty, by some strange mistake, exchanged his dispatches containing the treaty, for a bundle of old dispatches he met with at one of the post-offices between Washington and New Orleans, ordering out three regiments of militia. The mistake was not discovered until the seal was broken by general Jackson at headquarters.[41]

[40] *Niles' Weekly Register*, VIII (1815), 122.
[41] *Ibid.*

The unique note pictures the difficulties encountered by the dispatch carrier as he made his trip along the post road. Even with such handicaps mail moved with more precision than it had in the past.

In 1819 there appeared a notice concerning the routing of mail destined for the South. It was important that the dispatches be correctly directed in order that the shortest possible time be consumed in transportation. "All mails sent from the Atlantic states to Alabama, should be sent via Georgia, except to Huntsville, Somerville, Cotton Port, Athens, Marathon, and Florence; which, from the states north and east of South Carolina, should be sent in the Tennessee mail, via Knoxville, Ten."[42]

The people living in and around Nashville, Tennessee, were eager to have the stage line between Knoxville and Nashville supported so that the mail might pass through that section on its way to the West. A letter was addressed to Governor Joseph McMinn in 1819, in which the question of maintaining the road was considered. James Park and William Park wrote that "the support of a line of Stages from Knoxville to Nashville for the transportation of the mail and passengers is certainly desirable to the Citizens of this State and the more so when it is considered that on it depends the main western mail route to New Orleans being continued in that direction."[43]

Farther south interest was also manifested in post roads, especially those that connected the smaller communities with the larger settlements. In 1818 a post road was established from "Fort Mitchell, via . . . Fort Jackson, then by Mims Ferry to St. Stephens."[44] John James Audubon while in Natchez very carefully noted that "the mail arrived there

[42] *Ibid.*, XVII (1819-20), 441.
[43] Letter from James and Wm. Park to Joseph McMinn, Governor of Tennessee, October 2, 1819, Tennessee State Library, case no. 9.
[44] Elise Lathrop, *Early American Inns and Taverns*, p. 230.

The Relay. From *Stage Coach and Tavern Days*, by Alice Morse Earle.

thrice in the week from all parts of the Union."[45] In Florida a private mail route, which was to be a weekly mail, had been established between Claiborne, Alabama, and Pensacola. The places were eighty miles apart, and in order that the dispatches might be delivered quickly it was recommended that they be addressed "Pensacola, via Claiborne, Ala."[46] The condition in Cahawba with respect to the mails was given by Wm. Taylor, the postmaster, in the *Cahawba Press* under the caption "Arrivals and Departure of Mails."

Tuscaloosa mail closes at 9 o'clock, P. M. on Mondays, and departs Tuesday morning at 6 A. M., and returns every Saturday at 6 P. M. Claiborne mail closes same time and departs Tuesday at 12 o'clock, and returns every Sunday at 12 o'clock. Eastern or Georgia mail closes every Wednesday at 9 o'clock P. M., and departs Thursday morning at 6 o'clock, and returns every Wednesday at 6 o'clock P. M. East Tennessee mail closes every Monday at 9 o'clock, P. M., departs every Tuesday at 6 A. M., and returns every Sunday at 6 P. M.
Office open Sunday from 2 to 3.[47]

Weekly mails brought many problems. If the carriers did not make their connections as planned, the dispatches would lay over in the office until the mail went through the next week. A week's delay in mail that had already taken days and weeks to reach the South was of sufficient concern to everyone to force the Post Office authorities to alter the schedule.[48] Problems of this kind had to be corrected when they arose, for no one could look far enough into the future to be aware of impending difficulties.

In 1823 there were six distributing offices in the Old Southwest, Augusta, Georgia; Savannah, Georgia; Creek Agency, Georgia; St. Stephens, Alabama; Huntsville, Ala-

[45] Audubon, *op. cit.*, p. 333.
[46] *Niles' Weekly Register*, XX (1821), 272; XXI (1821-22), 80.
[47] *Cahawba Press and Alabama State Intelligencer*, III (1821-22), no. 26.
[48] *Ibid.*, no. 33.

bama; and Natchez, Mississippi.[49] These were the major points from which the post roads radiated forming a more or less complete network, becoming closer and closer woven as the years passed, bringing into the frontier sections new immigrants, who would in turn desire better mail facilities.

Postmasters of the distributing offices were required to open all mails directed to the state in which their offices were situated and to give the proper direction to each letter. All letters destined for places beyond the next distributing office were carefully enclosed in a strong envelope, and directed, so as to be conveyed on the most direct route, to their places of destination. They were placed in a portmanteau, the principal mail bag, which was opened and examined only at the distributing offices. An account was kept at each office of all the letters forwarded, and they were accompanied by post bills, in which were stated the charges for postage. Letters which were to be delivered at the offices between the distributing offices were placed in a separate portmanteau, called the way-bag, which was opened and examined by the postmasters of the intermediate offices.

To give greater security to the principal mails, locks entirely different from those used on the way-bags were placed on the portmanteaus, so that they could be opened without violence only at the distributing offices.[50]

This method of handling mail was expensive. The post office department paid at the rate of fifty-two dollars and seventy-six cents a mile for the transportation of mail, three trips a week, to New Orleans. Postmaster General McLean in a statement made on December 15, 1824, said that

> on a good turnpike road it could be conveyed in a stage as often, and in less than half the time, at the same expense. And, what is a more important consideration, the utmost security would be

[49] *American State Papers, Post Office*, p. 113.
[50] *Ibid.*

DEVELOPMENT OF POST ROADS 71

given to the mail by such a transportation, and a very considerable increase to the receipts of the Department.[51]

Settlement after settlement was linked up in this never ending chain of post roads. Over the roads plied the carrier, who was under contract to perform certain services. Mails were delayed, stage-coaches broken down, heavy rains made the roads impassable; yet the people of all the states demanded service, prompt service at any cost. The shortcomings of the mail contractors were quickly communicated to the Post Office Department, and, as a result, on January 15, 1825, Postmaster General John McLean issued a communication to all those who held contracts for carrying mail in the United States, in which letter he depicted some of the conditions to which they were to conform and the methods recommended by the Department.

The postmaster-general has observed, with great regret, that the exertions of some contractors, on important mail routes, have not equalled his expectation, or the expectation of the public.

This is the season when, to avoid failures, the utmost exertion of all concerned in the transportation of the mail are necessary. No obstacles, which human exertions can overcome, shall excuse a failure. Any want of energy, in this respect, will first be noticed by the highest pecuniary penalty; and, for a second failure the contract will be forfeited.

There will be no departure from this rule. Of this, those most interested may be fully assured.

On all the roads which become so deep as to render the rapid progress of stages impracticable, contractors are requested to place the mail in covered sulkies, or in other vehicles better suited for the purpose, and, in this manner, to continue the transportation of it, until the roads will admit of stages. Whatever may be the condition of the route, no trip should be lost.

The sudden rise of water-courses may stop the passage of the

[51] *Ibid.*, p. 120.

mail; bad roads cannot cause even the failure of a trip, if the proper means be applied with the necessary energy.

There are many roads where a stage, with six or eight passengers, and a large quantity of baggage, cannot travel five or six miles an hour; but there is no mail stage route in the union on which the mail cannot be conveyed in a sulky or cart, as rapidly as the contract requires. If two horses to a cart do not give sufficient force, four should be applied.

The transportation of the mail must not be made a secondary object—those who consider it in this light, will, very soon, be at liberty to bestow their undivided attention to the conveyance of passengers.[52]

The necessity of having the mails go through was thus brought to the attention of all those connected with the Post Office, whose coöperation was needed in order that the public might be served. A letter from Jane Wilkins, a resident of Natchez, to John Short of Lexington, Kentucky, illustrated but one occurrence of this inefficiency;

Your letter of January 5 this day (March 5) came to hand—so very irregular is the mail that I received yours of the 25th January a week sooner than the letter of a later date. Were it not for everybody complaining I should be led to believe it was a mistake in your date, but it is the case of all the arrivals here; the fault at present lies in the inattention of the post-masters and post riders. Be that as it may, the inhabitants of this place are great sufferers, particularly men of business.[53]

A contractor who did not have the energy or interest to carry on to the best of his ability was subject to dismissal.

Since the National Road, north of the Ohio River, was "now extending through Ohio, westward . . . rapidly,"[54] the South realized the value of such a road, and agitation was started for another National Road from Washington to

---

[52] *Niles' Weekly Register*, XXVII (1824-25), 341.
[53] Cincinnati *Enquirer Sunday Magazine*, March 25, 1923, p. 6.
[54] *Niles' Weekly Register*, XXIX (1825-26), 83.

New Orleans.[55] On April 30, 1823, an act was passed by Congress authorizing the President "to cause the necessary surveys, plans, and estimates to be made of the routes of such roads and canals as he may deem of national importance in a commercial or military point of view, or necessary to the transportation of the public mails."[56] As a consequence a communication was sent in February, 1825, from the Department of War to the Governor of Georgia. The letter was from J. C. Calhoun, notifying the Governor that a board of engineers was to visit his state to make an examination of a proposed route through Georgia. In Calhoun's words:

The board of engineers, for internal improvements, will leave ... between the 1st and 15th of the next month, for the purpose of commencing the examination of the several routes between the city of Washington and New Orleans, with a view of selecting the most eligible location for the great national road proposed to be established between those two points. The board will first make the examination of the route by the line of the capitals of the southern states, return by the intermediate route east of the mountains; thence, proceed back through the mountains. As it is a subject of great interest, both to the nation and the particular state through which the road may pass, it is very desirable, should it be convenient, that the civil engineer of the state should coöperate with the board, while examining the localities within the state, both going and returning; and, with the hope that you may concur in this view, you will be duly appraised of the place and probable time at which the board will enter the state, so that you may direct your engineers to meet the board, should you deem it advisable.[57]

Plans were well under way for the preliminary survey. The board would have to go over the ground and make a

[55] *American State Papers, Post Office*, pp. 119, 120.
[56] *Ibid., Military Affairs*, II, 699.
[57] *Niles' Weekly Register*, XXVIII (1825), 105.

detailed report of each route, and on the basis of this report a selection would be made. About a month and a half were consumed in making arrangements, and on April 16, 1825, a notice appeared in *Niles' Weekly Register* to the effect that the board had set out.

The board of engineers, consisting of General Bernard, Mr. Shriver, and the other officers and gentlemen attached to that service, set out, about a week since, on a tour of reconnaisance through the southern states, with a view of ascertaining the most eligible route for the contemplated national road from the seat of government to New Orleans.[58]

They had three routes to inspect: the Eastern Route, the Middle Route,[59] and the Western Route.[60] Each of these routes had its desirable features as well as the undesirable ones. In the following table[61] a few of the characteristics are compared:

	Eastern	Middle	Western
Material obtainable throughout	240 miles	752 miles	782 miles
Material scarce throughout	864 miles	354 miles	358 miles
Bridges— total length	6 mi. 626 yd.	5 mi. 491 yd.	3 mi. 953 yd.
Causeways— total length	35 mi. 586 yd.	39 mi. 356 yd.	24 mi. 1211 yd.

[58] *Ibid.*, p. 103; the membership of the board consisted of Brigadier General S. Bernard, and David Shriver, assisted by Captain W. T. Poussin, of the Topographical Engineers, Lieutenant G. Dutton, of the Corps of Engineers, and Lieutenant T. Trimble, of the Artillery. *House Documents*, 14th Congress, 1st Session, Document 156, p. 8.

[59] *Niles' Weekly Register*, XXIX (1825-26), 358.

[60] *American State Papers, Military Affairs*, III, 109, 137, 138; *Register of Debates*, 19th Congress, 1st Session, II (appendix), 18.

[61] Compiled from Report of General Bernard, *House Documents*, 19th Congress, 1st Session, Document 156; also quoted in *Niles' Weekly Register*, XXX (1826), 136.

DEVELOPMENT OF POST ROADS

Gradation	Eastern	Middle	Western
2°	785½ miles	714 miles	662 miles
3°	292¾ miles	324 miles	339 miles
4°	140¾ miles	166 miles	146½ miles
Population—			
White	202,430	262,335	204,295
Colored	210,284	164,632	107,899
Total	412,714	426,967	312,194
Distance from Washington to New Orleans from summary of reconnaisance	1,169 miles	1,204 miles	1,147½ miles
Probable distance—total	1,136 miles	1,108 miles	1,140 miles
At 2°	5/8	5/8	5/8
2° to 3°	3/8	3/8	3/8

It was necessary that they consider the value of each route to commerce, to the population they came in contact with, to defense, and to the transportation of mail.

Commerce. The eastern route would enjoy the exclusive advantage of facilitating the commercial correspondence between the inland importing and exporting marts. The middle and western would contribute more than the eastern to the development of internal commerce and industry.

Accommodation of Population. The eastern and middle routes would accommodate directly more states than the western; but taking into view, and by anticipation, the increase of population, perhaps the three routes ought to be placed on the same footing.

Defense. Through the western route, greater and more efficient assistance would be afforded in time of emergency to the states, and to naval establishments upon the gulf, than through the other routes.

Mail. General Bernard in his report said that "we are inclined to believe that the middle route has the advantage over the others" in respect to time. "As to expense, they will be less upon the middle, and especially upon the western; than upon the eastern. As to horses, the service of the mail will be better, and more cheaply secured upon the middle route, and especially upon the western, than upon the eastern."[62]

From these varied observations and comparisons it would seem that the middle route would be the most advantageous. Before making the final choice there was still one matter to be taken into consideration—the probable cost. "We must observe," said General Bernard, "that this estimate is far from being to us a satisfactory one: we are not provided with the minute survey and the local data in relation to the price of materials and labor. . . ."[63] The road was to be twenty-four feet in width; the summer road on each side, fourteen feet; each lateral ditch, four feet; which would give sixty feet for the breadth of the ground occupied by the road. The stone work on the road was to be fifteen inches in thickness.

Estimate.

	Eastern	Middle	Western
Road	$3,364,738.5	$4,325,703.7	$3,894,425
Bridges	1,570,800	1,240,800	572,000
Causeways	462,977.7	431,298.6	291,216
Total	5,398,516.2	5,997,802.3	4,757,641
Probable distance	1,136 mi.	1,106 mi.	1,140 mi.
Probable cost per mile	$4,752	$5,423	$4,173[64]

[62] *House Documents,* 19th Congress, 1st Session, Document 156, p. 26.
[63] *Ibid.,* Document 181, p. 5.
[64] Compiled from report of General Bernard, *House Documents,* 19th Congress, 1st Session, Document 181.

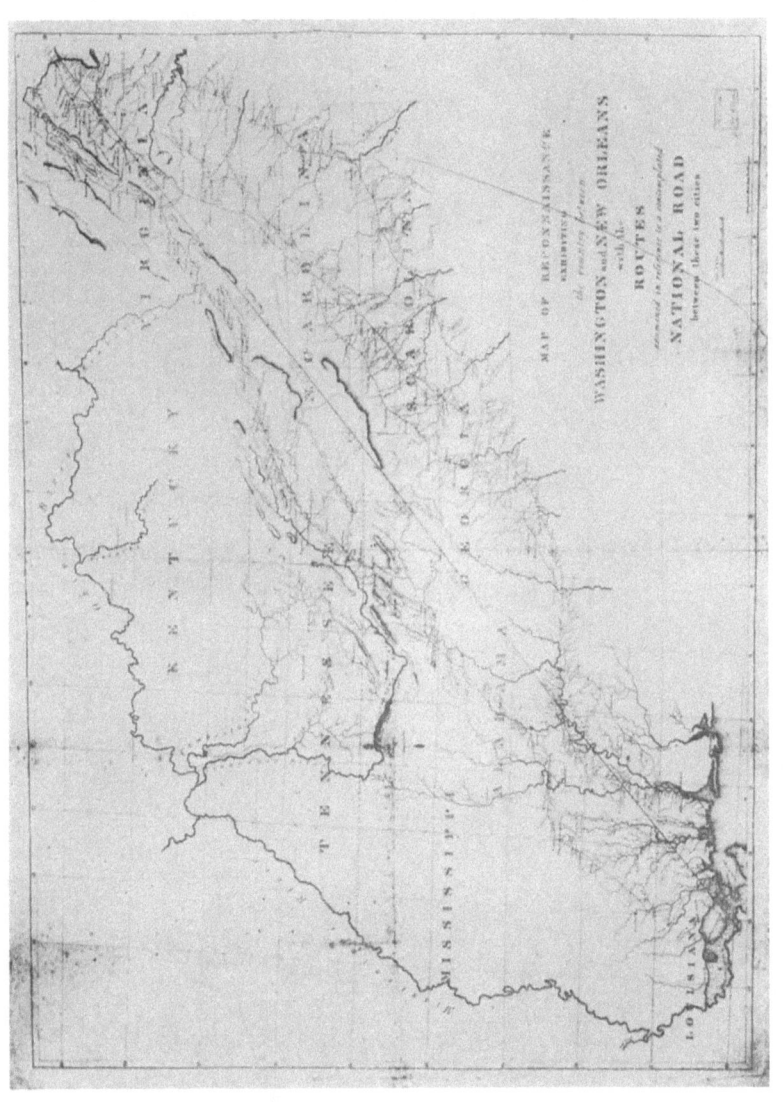

Proposed Routes Between Washington and New Orleans

In closing his report General Bernard stated that a national road, if so great an extent as that contemplated, from Washington to New Orleans, should not be commenced unless provisions be enacted before hand for its preservation. For, were not the sections or parts first finished carefully kept in repair, they would fall into decay soon after their construction, and there would be no end to the accomplishment of the whole work. In this respect, we beg leave to observe that, whilst the Post Office Department is enabled, by its regular correspondence, to receive full and timely information upon the condition of the roads, it is also more particularly interested in having them kept in good state of repair. Therefore, it seems to us that this Department might, with propriety, be entrusted with this branch of public service. Such an arrangement, besides removing all collision which, otherwise, might arise between this Department and any other entrusted with the repair of our National Roads, would, at the same time, place at its disposal all the means upon which more especially depend the rapid and regular transportation of the mail along these roads.[65]

His report was submitted to the House of Representatives[66] on April 11, 1826, by James Barbour, Secretary of War, and the next day it was referred to the Committee on Roads and Canals. Its history while in committee is not certain, but in the report of the Secretary of War, sent to the President on November 26, 1827, and communicated to Congress with his address on December 4, 1827, the opening of the 20th Congress, he explained that the survey had been made, that the report had been submitted to the 19th Congress, and that no further step could "be taken by the department till the pleasure of Congress is signified by legislative enactment."[67]

During this period two routes were employed by the

[65] *House Documents,* 19th Congress, 1st Session, Document 156, pp. 27, 28.
[66] *American State Papers, Military Affairs,* III, 616.
[67] *Ibid.*

postal authorities in transporting mail from Washington to New Orleans. The first went from Washington through Abingdon, Knoxville, Columbia, and Natchez to New Orleans and required twenty-four to twenty-five days to cover. The second, which corresponded closely to the eastern route investigated by the army, went by way of the capitals of the Southern States, then through Montgomery to Mobile, from which point the mail was carried by steamer one hundred and seventy miles to New Orleans. The eastern "route was considerably shorter than that by way of Abingdon and Knoxville and the Department calculated that it could be negotiated in 19 days if the necessary bridges were provided."[68] Postmaster General McLean estimated that a good turnpike road would allow service in eleven days, but would cost the government $50,000 a year for the three trips a week. "In 1829 Postmaster General Barry reported that the next year would see in operation a service three times a week, by way of Augusta, Georgia, Montgomery, and Mobile. The whole trip was to be accomplished in two weeks."[69]

With regular, established mail service in the South the territory became more desirable to home seekers. While the earlier penetration was mainly done by traders, who had their homes and basis for operation on the coast in the older and more densely settled areas, the immigration that followed was of a different type. The new immigrant was in search of a home. He sought out a location, cleared the land, erected his cabin, and became identified with the frontier.

[68] Wesley Everett Rich, *History of the United States Post Office to the Year 1829*, p. 84.
[69] *Ibid.*

CHAPTER V
THE TRAVELER ON THE ROAD

FOR THE BEST picture of actual conditions of trade, travel, and communication during the first quarter of the nineteenth century, we must turn to the accounts of travelers. The immigrants themselves, for obvious reasons, were too absorbed in their struggle with frontier conditions to write much concerning those conditions. It was the traveler, with the detached and somewhat patronizing attitude of the transient observer and the realism with which one views matters pertaining to his own comfort, who has given us the most accurate as well as the most interesting accounts of conditions prevailing on the travel and trade routes around the southern end of the Appalachians.

Judge Walton in a speech to a grand jury of Wilkes County in 1785 made an interesting statement; ". . . I look forward to a time, not far distant, when . . . the whole (of Georgia) will be settled and connected . . . from the shore of the Atlantic to the banks of the Mississippi."[1] This represents the trend of thought of those on the Atlantic coast and it gave impetus to those that were developing the means of transportation. Men with a far-sighted vision were the prophets of the new age in modes of travel.

John Melish, when traveling in Georgia during the year 1806, noted that the road was "pretty good" and ran through a hilly, uncultivated tract of country.[2]

Adam Hodgson, in the spring of 1820, journeyed from Augusta to New Orleans over the Middle Trading Path. One week previous to his departure from Augusta he had

[1] Whitaker, *op. cit.*, p. 6, quoted from *Gazette of the State of Georgia*, April 14, 1785.
[2] *Travels Through the United States of America*, p. 50.

traveled by stage from Savannah.³ He purchased a horse for himself and one for his servant and set out on the 17th of March with the intention of proceeding overland to Mobile or New Orleans.⁴ The next evening they met three rough back-woodsmen who had come from the Mississippi over the same route they had planned to take. The strangers came "with a wretched account of the roads; the bridges over the creeks having been almost all washed away, and the swamps being nearly impassable."⁵ The frontiersmen strongly urged Hodgson not to attempt the expedition. On the following day they met two more travelers who were "quite exhausted" and they told the same story of bad roads adding "that for many days they had to swim their horses over most of the flooded creeks on the road. . ."⁶ Hodgson arrived at Fort Hawkins on March 21, and toward evening they "passed six waggons, conveying ninety slaves, belonging to General ———— removing from his plantation in Georgia, to his settlement on the Cahawba, in Alabama."⁷ The next day as they proceeded from Fort Hawkins, they passed several more wagons of emigrants from Georgia and Carolina moving on to Alabama. There were "many gangs of slaves whom their masters were transporting to Alabama and Mississippi and . . . one party returning from New Orleans to Georgia."⁸ During the day they did not pass a single house or settlement; the pine avenue was without interruption for thirty miles. On the 23rd they joined an Alabama cotton-planter and his daughter, who were returning from Milledgeville, where the daughter had been in school. They travelled in a little Jersey waggon (or dearborn, or carry-all, as this humble vehicle is variously denominated,)—'camping out' every night and cooking their bacon

---

³ *Op. cit.*, I, 103.
⁴ *Ibid.*, p. 106.
⁵ *Ibid.*, p. 110.
⁶ *Ibid.*, p. 110.
⁷ *Ibid.*, p. 113.
⁸ *Ibid.*, p. 114.

and coffee three times a day."⁹ The following day they set out as soon as it was light and passing several creeks, they arrived at the extremity of the ridge, from which they "looked down into a savannah, in which was situated the Indian town of Ce-se-ta, on the Chatahouchy."¹⁰ Hodgson in his letters said that "the surface of the ground continues to form a perpetual undulation. The road, which is called the Federal Road, though tolerable for horses, would to us be considered impassable for wheels."¹¹ As they proceeded they passed as usual many large parties of emigrants from South Carolina and Georgia, and many gangs of slaves. There seemed to be a continuous procession westward.

Point Comfort was the next point on the road, and after passing this place they saw a fine cotton plantation. Seeing the highly cultivated fields they realized that they were no longer traveling through a nation of hunters. The "road, which had hitherto been generally excellent for travelling on horseback, became wretchedly bad."¹² They had to pass through three swamps, and it was estimated that the fatigue of crossing any of them would equal at least fifteen or twenty miles of common traveling. On and on the traveler advanced. In describing this stage of the journey, Hodgson said that "our road again lay through a most solitary pine barren, on a high ridge. The only thing which attracted my attention during the morning, was a finger-post of wood fastened to a tree and pointing down a grass path, and on which was written 'To Pensacola'."¹³ From Augusta to Mobile, the way they came, was about four hundred and sixty miles, which was accomplished in about fifteen days, of which time they rested two days.

A few years later General Lafayette traveled over this

⁹ *Ibid.*, p. 120.
¹⁰ *Ibid.*, p. 121.
¹¹ *Ibid.*, p. 126.
¹² *Ibid.*, p. 139.
¹³ *Ibid.*, p. 145.

road. In the account of the journey, written by his secretary, the roads were described as being in bad condition, and very much broken up. The party was traveling in carriages; but as the travelers proceeded, many of them had to resort to horseback. "The first day the jolts were so violent that they occasioned General Lafayette a vomiting which alarmed 'all of the party' but this entirely ceased after a good night passed at Warrenton."[14]

Every type of road was encountered. One was described as "a kind of gulley or fissure, over the bottom of which the General's carriage was drawn with difficulty, and often at the risk of being shattered in pieces."[15] The farther west the party advanced the more difficult the roads became. The entire trip was outlined in a communication to Jefferson in which Lafayette said, "I am on my way to Norfolk from thence to proceed to Raleigh, Fayetteville, to South Carolina, Georgia, and by land to Montgomery where a steamboat will take us to Mobile and New Orleans: I shall after four days stay at New Orleans visit all the states up the Mississippi and Ohio."[16]

From these accounts it may be seen that the road had not been improved. In many places it was still almost impassable. These men were describing actual conditions; therefore their accounts form a good basis for judgment.

Years passed; thousands of people moved over the roads. Each year saw new improvements made, yet all of them were temporary in nature, for none of the travel accounts mentioned any lasting improvements.

In the year 1831, Thomas Hamilton journeyed over the same route, but in the other direction, this time from Mobile to Augusta. He described the road by saying that "our road

[14] A. Levasseur, *Lafayette in America in 1824 and 1825*, II, 66, 67.
[15] *Ibid.*, pp. 70, 71.
[16] *Letters of Lafayette and Jefferson*, p. 431.

was what is expressively called a natural one, and lay through a continuous pine forest."[17] When his party reached Line Creek they found a ferry boat, onto which they ran the coach, and by means of a hawser stretched across the river the ferry was drawn to the opposite shore, from which they proceeded. Hamilton said,

I have had occasion to say a great deal about roads in these volumes, but I pronounce that along which our route lay on the present occasion to be positively, comparatively, and superlatively the *very worst* I have ever travelled in the whole course of my peregrinations. The ruts were axle-deep, and there were occasionally huge crevices, in which, but for great strategy on the part of the coachman, the vehicle must have been engulfed.[18]

The road was continuous through a pine forest. To relieve the horses the party was compelled to walk. Then for some distance the road became better, being composed of sand without stones. It was heavy for the horses but was not uncomfortable for the passengers.

After leaving Fort Mitchell, they crossed the Chattahoochee and entered the state of Georgia. They continued to pass through an almost unbroken pine forest, having more sand roads in which the wheels sank up to the axles.[19] They proceeded to Augusta after many varied experiences.

Charles Joseph Latrobe traveled through southern Georgia, where he found the same conditions. In his account he continually complained of "the difficulty of travelling."[20] He journeyed through the pine barrens "over a road which our canny borderer had described to us as, 'a very fairish sort of a road,'—one in which the stumps are cut pretty nigh level, that is, within two feet of the ground."[21] Latrobe was very definite in his statements concerning the roads. He

[17] *Men and Manners in America*, p. 360.
[18] *Ibid.*, p. 369. [19] *Ibid.*, pp. 378, 379.
[20] *The Rambler in North America*, II, 42.
[21] *Ibid.*, p. 53.

said, "The roads through the south of Georgia are in the roughest state,"[22] continuing, "From all this you may gather that travelling in the South is still in its infancy, and I may add shamefully expensive. You pay exorbitantly for the meanest fare."[23] From the southern part of Georgia he went north until he arrived at Milledgeville on the Middle Trading Path. "At this town we got into the great line of interior communication between the Southern States, and took advantage of the Piedmont line of Stages, to move northward to the frontiers of North Carolina, where we turned aside with the purpose of crossing Alleghany to Knoxville in Tennessee."[24]

The territory west of the Creek Nations had as its focal point Mobile, which was situated at the head of Mobile Bay and in a position to benefit from all the trade of the Alabama and Tombigbee Rivers. As the hordes of immigrants came into this section, they settled on the choice land as would a flock of hungry birds on a field of grain. Always the land that was not available looked the finest, and in this case the land held by the Indians was the land that they wanted. In the Nashville *Clarion* there appeared the following article:

Imagination looks forward to the movement when all the Southern Indians shall be pushed across the Mississippi: when the delightful countries now occupied by them shall be covered with a numerous and industrious population; and when a city, the emporium of a vast commerce, shall be seen to flourish on the spot where some huts, inhabited by lawless savages, now mark the juncture of the Alabama and Tombigbee rivers.[25]

Of the people who settled on the shores of the Mobile Bay large numbers were adherents of the British cause, who

[22] *Ibid.*, p. 63.
[23] *Ibid.*, p. 64.   [24] *Ibid.*, p. 71.
[25] *Niles' Weekly Register*, III (1812), 53, quoted from Nashville (Tenn.) *Clarion*.

had fled thither through the trackless forests from South Carolina and Georgia during the early days of the Revolution.[26]

The Alabama country had numerous local roads in addition to the main road from Georgia to New Orleans. One of the most important, running in a general southwestward direction, was the Military Road. It was considered one of the finest in the Union and was opened under the direction of General Andrew Jackson. According to a contemporary account:

> Houses of entertainment have been erected at short stages to render every comfort to the traveler. This road runs thro' a delightful and romantic country, and must eventually become the great thoroughfare to the Southern states. In travelling the road, the men of pleasure will find a rich repast served up for contemplation, and the man of business every facility to expedite his journey. The day is not far distant when a line of stages will be established from Nashville to New Orleans, which must necessarily render the military road the most important of any on the continent.
>
> Independent of the great advantage this road possesses over the old 'trace' (as it is called) it lessens the distance to New Orleans more than 300 miles.[27]

Though the Military Road ran north and south connecting two distant points in the western territory, it served the immigrants as they made their way West by assisting them to reach other highways that would lead them toward the Mississippi River. There was the ever-present problem of supplies, especially while the men of the household were erecting the cabin. "The sudden and very numerous emigration into the Alabama country threaten many with absolute

---

[26] W. H. Siebert, "The Loyalists in West Florida and the Natchez District," *Mississippi Valley Association Proceedings*, VIII (1914-15), 103.

[27] *Niles' Weekly Register*, XIX (1820-21), 80.

starvation, unless they are shortly relieved by supplies from other parts."²⁸

The *Western Gazetteer* mentioned that in 1817 the town of Blakely was situated at the mouth of the Tensaw River, on the east side of Mobile Bay. A good road could be found along the dividing ridge separating the branches of the Conecah and Escambia Rivers from those of the Alabama; and the distance from Mobile to Fort Claiborne, by this route, was thirty miles shorter than by that of St. Stephens. The account continued that "the main road from Georgia to New Orleans will probably strike Mobile Bay at this point (Blakely)."²⁹

From St. Stephens the roads led in many directions over high dry lands, and could be traveled at all seasons without extraordinary difficulty. Darby had words of instruction for immigrants. "Persons intending to visit the valley of the Mobile, ought to depart from their place of outset, so as to arrive in the country in November or December. The winter is the most agreeable and safest season for newcomers in any part of the United States south of 35° N. Lat."³⁰ In regard to the road to New Orleans he said that it "can be traveled at all seasons of the year, and this route is only embarrassed by having Lake Pontchartrain to pass. There is no considerable difficulty, however, in passing that lake, as packet schooners daily ply from New Orleans to Madisonville."³¹

Public conveyances were not yet established in the Mississippi and Mobile countries by the year 1818. Travelers were obliged to provide for themselves the means of transportation. Horses of all prices were constantly to be procured in

---

²⁸ *Ibid.*, XII (1817), 96.
²⁹ *Western Gazetteer*, p. 16.
³⁰ William Darby, *The Emigrant's Guide to the Western and Southwestern States and Territories*, p. 38.
³¹ *Ibid.*

New Orleans, Natchez, and other points, a medium price being about eighty dollars.[32]

Notwithstanding the impossibility of procuring public transportation, people continued to enter the territory. Governor William W. Bibb, in an address to the Legislative Council and House of Representatives of Alabama, discussed the question of roads:

Permit me to recommend to the attention of the legislature the subject of roads, ferries, and bridges. The strength of a country consists in its population and it is peculiarly the interest of this territory to invite emigration hither, by furnishing every possible facility of communication. I am aware, however, that under existing circumstances the object cannot be wholly attained without the interposition of the government of the U. States.[33]

There was probably no portion of the world, of similar extent, which could exhibit such an astonishingly rapid increase in population, produced by the voluntary emigration of enterprising individuals.[34]

There were always a great many hazards encountered by a traveler on the road. The Indian, whose territory he was penetrating, was an ever-present menace to the immigrant.[35] General Mitchell, in a communication to William Rabun, Governor of Georgia, said:

I understand that much apprehension prevails about the safety with which travellers can pass through the nation. It is my opinion there is not the least danger in traveling the road from Fort Hawkins to the Alabama, by this place (Creek Agency) and fort Mitchell, but I would not advise travellers to use the road from fort Perry to fort Gaines; or indeed any road as low down as fort Gaines, for the present.[36]

[32] *Ibid.*, p. 43.
[33] *Niles' Weekly Register*, XIV (1818), 44.
[34] *Ibid.*, XXVII (1824-25), 259, 260.
[35] *Ibid.*, V (1813-14), 270, 271, 282, 283, 284; XIV (1818), 270; XV (1818-19), 91, 125; XXIII (1822-23), 48.
[36] *Ibid.*, XIII, (1817-18), 390.

From this statement it can be seen that the road along the fall line was considered the best and safest. Though this was true, G. W. Featherstonhough had a great amount of trouble going over the road in 1835. Before starting on his journey to Georgia, he inquired about the conditions within the Indian Nation. He was told that the road was excessively broken up, that the Indian bridges were out, and that in consequence thereof, the mail coaches could not go through, the mail being forwarded on horseback. As a result of this condition he had to secure private conveyance and pay any price the owner thought proper to ask. A coach was secured and arrangements were made to start. They

found the road as we advanced quite answering to the description they had given us of it, being so frightfully cut up as to render it impossible to sit in the vehicle: wherever it was dry enough, therefore, we walked expecting every instant to see the carriage overturned; and indeed the manner in which it survived the rolling from one side to the other was quite surprising. The black fellow, however, who drove us seemed to take it as philosophically as if there was nothing uncommon in this sort of motion; he always urged us in a very anxious manner to get in whenever he came up with us, and seemed to think we were not quite right in our senses for preferring to walk when we paid so much for riding. At length we came to a low part of the country completely inundated, where it was impossible to walk, the water being in many places four feet deep. Here we were obliged to get in, and the old vehicle took to rolling in such a dreadful manner that every instant we expected to be soused into the water; and what rendered it really amusing was, that we were constantly obliged to draw up our limbs on the seat, for the water was at least eight inches deep in the bottom in the most extraordinary manner. All this time our trunks, which were lashed on behind, were being quietly dragged under the water.[37]

[37] G. W. Featherstonhough, *Excursion through the Slave States*, II, 285.

Numerous local roads connected isolated communities, such as: the Gaines Trace,[38] Bolivar Indian Trail,[39] Natchez Trace,[40] and Robinson Road.[41] The road connecting Mobile and Pensacola[42] was not long but was of major importance, for both settlements were of commercial significance. Hundreds of others were in existence at this time, and each one provided a new avenue of penetration into the western territory.[43] The short period between the coming of the early settlers and the time the district became a state attests the desirability of the land, the eagerness of the immigrants, and the ease of transportation.

"The first stage route east from Montgomery was established by Lewis Calfrey and Major James W. Johnston, at one time proprietors of the inn at Fort Mitchell, and by 1823, two trips each way were made weekly."[44] Public conveyances were not common in 1828, when Colonel Albert James Pickett, then a young man, decided to attend a military school in Connecticut. He left his home on "horseback, with a pair of saddle-bags, which contained something to eat as well as something to wear, and travelled . . . through the territory inhabited by various tribes of Indians, who were in a state of almost open hostility because of the efforts of the Federal Government to obtain their land. . . ."[45]

Such were the conditions in the basin of the Alabama and the Tombigbee Rivers during the early years of the

[38] George J. Leftwich, "Some Main Travelled Roads, Including Cross Sections of Natchez Trace," *Mississippi Historical Society Publications,* Centenary Series, I (1916), 467.

[39] *Ibid.,* pp. 467, 468.

[40] *Ibid.,* pp. 465, 466.

[41] *Ibid.,* pp. 466, 467.

[42] *Niles' Weekly Register,* VII (1814-15), supplement, 105-7.

[43] Cf. map *18th Annual Report, Bureau American Ethnology,* pt. 2, 1896; *The American Military Pocket Atlas,* map no. 5, "The Southern Colonies."

[44] Lathrop, *op. cit.,* p. 233.

[45] Michael Leonard Woods, *Personal Reminiscences of Colonel Albert James Pickett,* p. 598.

nineteenth century. It may be seen that there was not a great amount of variance between this section and Georgia.

The territory west of Alabama was of the same general character. "In 1785 a citizen of Augusta wrote that 'a vast number' of the upland settlers were removing toward the Mississippi in consequence of the relinquishment of Natchez by the Spaniards."[46] The immigrants as described by one present at the time were

> either men of fortune, or needy adventurers. The middle classes, having from 2 to 3,000 dollars worth of property, seldom chose to settle there, having no prospect of succeeding by dint of personal industry. . . . Most of the respectable settlers are therefore from Virginia, Tennessee, Georgia, the Carolinas, and Kentucky; having sold their property there, and emigrated with their slaves into this country.[47]

Traveling as far as they did, the emigrants came in contact with many of the Indians, and their relations became somewhat tense. Benjamin Hawkins addressed to Governor Claiborne a communication in which he discussed the question. He said that

> it is much to be wished that the people of this territory could be prevailed on to observe a friendly deportment toward the Indians particularly on occasions like the present; as all intercourse by land between us and the Atlantic States is through the Indian Lands, a disposition on their part unfriendly toward travellers would greatly incommode them.[48]

An early account, dated 1785, stated that it was "reported that a thousand families are ready to come down as soon as the boundaries are known."[49] They entered the territory over the same routes that have been described,

---
[46] Phillips, *op. cit.*, p. 171; cf. *South Carolina Gazette*, May 26, 1785.
[47] *Americans as They Are*, pp. 140, 141.
[48] *Official Letter Books of W. C. C. Claiborne*, I, 21.
[49] "Papers relating to Bourbon County, Georgia," *American Historical Review*, XV (1910), 97.

undergoing the same hardships, and finally experiencing the same joys when settled on their own land. Roads were established and towns founded. The Natchez Trace was quite well known, but its direction was generally north and south and therefore did not greatly facilitate westward travel. William Darby in 1818, said that for several years previously a stage had been running between New Orleans and Baton Rouge but was discontinued for want of sufficient encouragement.[50] Fortescue Cuming described this country as being broken up, and as he went farther south it became "more broken, but the soil improved, and the road degenerating to a bridle path through the woods, and being hilly and forked and intersected by cattle paths, was both difficult to find and disagreeable to travel."[51] Continuing, he said that "the road, which had been opened wide enough for a wagon, but now much overgrown by poke and other high weeds, ... led ... along the top of a narrow and very crooked ridge. ..."[52] It was "impossible to travel in any part of this new country after dark, as the roads are only bridle paths, which are so darkened by the woods through which they lead, that the adventurous traveller must inevitably lose himself."[53]

During the early days of settlements in the Mississippi region, Montfort Browne, acting governor of West Florida, wrote to the Earl of Hillsbrough concerning the desirability of settlements on the Mississippi River.

I am of opinion my Lord that a Town Ship shou'd be laid out at or near Natchez or at some convenient place on the River and that a good road be opened from the settlement of Mobile to the town so laid out. Nothing can forward the Settlement of a new Place more than this, Especially in a Country destitute of Inhabitants and so worthy of being inhabited. Indeed at present there

[50] *Op. cit.*, p. 43.
[51] *Sketches of a Tour to the Western Country*, p. 287.
[52] *Ibid.*, p. 288.   [53] *Ibid.*, p. 314.

is a political necessity for taking these steps, for a great part of the immense Indian trade which comes from near Detroit down our side of the Mississippi principally centers at New Orleans.[54]

The political necessity that he mentioned was of course brought about by the struggle between France and England. Commercial rivalry was strong between these powers, as was emphasized in Chapter II.

Immigration into the western section of the southern area was relatively slow until about 1770, notwithstanding the advertisement for settlers, the efforts of officials in charge of the country, and the land speculators who wanted to induce people to settle and improve the land. These and other forces were at work, but less obviously and more slowly than had been the case in the earlier settlements. Allan B. Magruder, in a letter dated 1807, said that "emigration to Louisiana will be more gradual than it was to the countries on the Ohio. . . . The principal part of lower Louisiana will be settled by the slave-holder from the southern part of the United States."[55]

New Orleans was the most important center in southern Louisiana. In 1784 Thomas Hutchins remarked that "there is reason to believe the period is not very distant when New Orleans may become a great and opulent city, if we consider the advantages of its situation. . . ."[56] John Pope, who was there in the year 1791, described it as being

the Residence of Don Miro a Spanish viceroy, and Emporium of Louisiana and the Indian Territories dependent thereon— It lies in almost an exact Square. The Streets which are wide and some of them well paved with Brick, intersect each other at right

---

[54] Clarence E. Carter, "Some Aspects of British Administration in West Florida," *Mississippi Valley Historical Review*, I (1914), 369.

[55] Allan B. Magruder, *A Letter from Allan B. Magruder, Esq. of Opelousas, to his Correspondent in the State of Virginia, Dated 20th November 1807*, p. 15.

[56] *An Historical Narrative and Topographical Description of Louisiana, and West Florida*, p. 37.

angles. The public Buildings are capacious and elegant. The private Houses generally neat and commodious.[57]

A few years later (1802) Berquin-Duvallon was traveling in Louisiana and recorded his impressions of New Orleans:

it deserved rather the name of a great straggling town, than of a city; though even to merit that title, it would be required to be larger. In fact, the mind can, I think, scarcely image to itself a more disagreeable place on the face of the whole globe; it is disgusting in what ever point of view it be contemplated, both as a whole, separately, and the wild, brutish aspect of its suburbs; yet it is the only town in the whole colony, and, in the ardour of admiration, it is called by the inhabitants the capitol, the city.[58]

He concluded by saying: "It must however be acknowledged that New Orleans is destined by nature to become one of the principal cities of North America, and perhaps the most important place of commerce in the new world, if it can only maintain the incalculable advantage of being the sole *entrepot* and central point of a country almost flat. . . ."[59] During the years that followed, Louisiana became a part of the United States, a new tide of immigration flooded into this section, and the general aspect changed. It became the center of a settled community. Jabez W. Heustis made some observations in 1816 in which he said that "the side-walks are paved with bricks, but the middle of the street is not paved. This neglect is a material inconvenience to the city. . . ."[60] The following year did not witness many internal improvements in New Orleans. Commenting on this, Darby said: "the streets are not yet paved;

---

[57] *A Tour through the Southern and Western Territories of the United States,* p. 37.
[58] *Travels in Louisiana and the Floridas,* p. 35.
[59] *Ibid.*
[60] *Physical Observations,* p. 25.

though a paved footway lines most streets in front of the houses, with gutters to carry away the surplus water."[61]

To this embryonic metropolis all roads led. It seemed to be the center to which all life gravitated. The roads immediately around New Orleans were soon to be in need of repairs, as were those in all parts of the South. Reconditioning them was indispensable to the whole country, and it was requested that a detail of regular soldiers be sent to make the needed improvements.[62] As a measure of defense the army kept many of the roads in good condition, for any section without serviceable highways was difficult to defend, and the Old Southwest was no exception.

Francois Xavier Martin, an historian living in New Orleans, wrote to his friend Colonel John Hamilton of Elizabeth City, North Carolina, telling him of the country on the Mississippi River and instructing him concerning the routes that could be traveled between the two cities. The letter in part is as follows:

Your son has not deceived you in the idea he has given of the banks of the Mississippi. There are I believe no lands in the U. S. that repay so richl(y) the toils of the husbandman. . . . If you contemplate a removal I dare (say) you cannot do better than coming over. . . .

Intending to visit the river the best season in the year is to start the first of September from your house, . . .

If you preferred a Souther(n) rout you might come to Athens or Milledgeville in Georgia thence to Col. Ben Hawkins, the Indian Agent among the Creek(s)—thence to Fort Stoddart—& thence to Natchez—this route is between 2 or 200 miles nearer (than the route through Tennessee) but you have a greater portion of Indian country to travel thro'—the nation(s) you pass

---

[61] *A Geographical Description of the State of Louisiana, the Southern part of the State of Mississippi, and Territory of Alabama*, p. 74; for a description of New Orleans in 1827 see *Americans as They Are*, pp. 152-218.

[62] *American State Papers, Indian Affairs*, II, 80.

thro' are less civilized, the road worse and less travelled and the water courses frequent and much wider.[63]

By word of mouth and by letters, people in the East were being influenced to sell their holdings, pack the necessities of life in wagons, and start the trek westward. The route that most of them selected was the one that followed the fall line across the Southern states. It afforded easy transportation, a minimum number of broad streams, and only a few swamps to cross. "Ease in travel" must not be misunderstood, for it was easy only when it was compared with the journeys of de Soto and other early discoverers.

A traveller intending to proceed thence (from Augusta) by land to New Orleans is earnestly recommended to bid adieu to all comforts on leaving Augusta, and make the necessary preparations for a hard and rough campaign. If he has a wife and children unprovided for, and to whom he has not the means of leaving a suitable legacy, let him by all means be careful to insure his life to the highest amount the office will take; for the chances of perishing on the road are at the rate of ten to one.[64]

Although this statement was made in 1832, conditions were not greatly improved, notwithstanding the fact that many roads had been opened, bridges built, taverns constructed, and causeways thrown across swamps.

Carl Arfwedson had planned to journey from Augusta to New Orleans and everyone had warned him of the innumerable hazards which would be encountered on the trip. In his words:

I could not refrain from laughing, satisfied in my own mind that they were exaggerated, and that I could not possibly have to endure more than I had already encountered during my

[63] *Documentary History of American Industrial Society*, II, 192-200.
[64] C. D. Arfwedson, *The United States and Canada, in 1832, 1833, and 1834*, I, 413, 414.

journey from Norfolk to Charleston; but experience soon taught me to view the latter trip in the light of pleasant and comfortable, when compared with the inconveniences, not to say sufferings, to which a traveller is exposed, when hazarding his person in the woods of Georgia and Alabama. I had hitherto ventured to indulge in invectives against the roads in Virginia and both Carolinas: these were now English turnpike-roads, when compared with those I had actually to traverse. I had also complained of the indifference of the stages in the same State: in Alabama I should have deemed myself happy, could I but have got sight of a Virginia stage, instead of the skeleton vehicles which were presented to my view. Too often had I heaped animadversions on the Virginia drivers: in Alabama again, I should have conferred on them the title of real gentlemen. I had even gone so far as to speak in derision and with contempt of the tough, split, and broiled fowls, with which a traveller is regaled at every meal in Virginia, and which are alive five minutes before they are put on the table for consumption: in Alabama, where bacon and sweet potatoes constitute the only delicacies, one of the feathered tribe would have been considered superior to the best Parisian pateé aux truffes.[65]

In 1831 there appeared in the Augusta *Constitutionalist* an article describing frontier conditions, which serves to substantiate the foregoing statements:

The inhabitants of our city are scarcely aware that there exist within one hundred miles of them people peculiar in habits, persuits, and manners, and among whom the absence of refinement and luxury is compensated by a republican simplicity—native vigor of intellect—the kindness of heart. . . . The country is wild, sparsely settled, full of game, and if we except one or two highways leading to Savannah, almost without roads, the paths dignified by the name of roads being almost overgrown by grass, and so dim and blind that the traveller almost unconsciously wanders from them into the forests. . . .[66]

[65] *Ibid.*, pp. 414, 415.
[66] Augusta (Ga.) *Constitutionalist*, October 18, 1831, quoted in *Documentary History of American Industrial Society*, II, 167.

These travelers all verified frontier conditions still existing in the states of Georgia, Alabama, Mississippi, and Louisiana after the first quarter of the nineteenth century. This was the period that saw the introduction of the railroads. Mrs. Dunbar Rowland described the different types of routes that extended through the South as "including water, stage-coach and detached lines of new railroads. . . ."[67]

[67] Eron Opha Rowland, *Varina Howell, Wife of Jefferson Davis*, I, 138.

CHAPTER VI
INNS AND TAVERNS OF THE OLD SOUTH

THE SUBJECT of "Inns and Taverns in the Old South" always brings to mind one of two scenes: the first, an iron-balconied brick building in New Orleans—people moving in and out—on the inside, music—on the outside, sunshine or rain. There is always movement—the slow languid step of the French creole, the shuffle of the negro, or the brisk but heavy tread of the Yankee trader just up from the river. People are everywhere—the hotel or inn is the gathering place for all: the trader, the adventurer, the servant, the pleasure-seeker, and those of more questionable character. This is one scene that flashes through one's mind when he thinks of a tavern in a Southern city. The other scene is of a rural tavern. It is approached on horse-back or in a carriage. One enters through a long tree-lined drive, at the end of which the high pillared verandah invites the traveler to tarry awhile, have a mint julep, and discuss the affairs of the day. There is a certain solemnity about it all, nothing to hurry one. The quiet restfulness of this inn is typical of the Southern plantation and in marked contrast to the tavern of the city. These are just two of the many pictures that might be brought to mind by the words "Inns and Taverns in the Old South." Are they true? Have they any basis in fact? Or, are they images that have been built up as an ideal? The last is nearest the fact. On examination it may be found that scenes such as have been described existed only in isolated cases.

The great majority of the inns and taverns in the South were neither comfortable nor picturesque. The name seemed to mean little, as a traveler noted in 1784 when he remarked that

> there is no distinction here between inns, taverns, ordinaries, and public-houses; they are all in one, and are known by the appelation of taverns, public-houses, or ordinaries, which, in the general acceptance of the name here, are synomymous terms. They are very indifferent indeed, compared with the inns in England; and three-fourths of them are in reality little better than mere shelters from the weather; yet the worst of them is by by no means deficient in charging high.[1]

The Southern planter was by nature eager to entertain guests. Bishop Hoss was quoted as saying that "Light, stranger, hitch your horse and come in," was the usual salutation used when anybody came to the door that was not known by face.[2] The readiness to entertain that existed in the Southern states made taverns less necessary than in the North. Francis Baily, making a tour through the South, "observed that there are few taverns in these newly-settled countries; but that almost all the farmers who lived near the road will take in strangers and travellers, giving them what is called 'dry entertainment'; that is, board and lodging but without any spiritous liquors."[3]

These private homes, in addition to those established by an agreement with the Creek Indians, constituted the rural inns. "The Creek Indians' treaty stipulated that 'stopping places for travelers through the Nation be provided.' These were between thirteen and sixteen miles apart, and the government regulated the charge for meals as follows: breakfast, fifty cents; dinner and supper, seventy-five cents."[4] Travelers all agreed in their opinion of the inns, and a great

[1] J. F. D. Smyth, *A Tour in the United States of America*, I, 50.
[2] Maxine Mathews, "Old Inns in East Tennessee," *East Tennessee Historical Society Publications*, II (1930), 22.
[3] *Ibid.*, pp. 22, 23.
[4] Lathrop, *op. cit.*, pp. 229, 230.

many pages were devoted to describing the wretched conditions which prevailed in the average hut, "called a tavern,"[5] as one man expressed it.

In Savannah the first tavern was in operation within a year after the founding of the settlement (1733), as was shown on the early map of the town drawn by Peter Gordon. This establishment was known as the "House for Strangers."[6] As the population increased and the need became greater other houses were opened. The great variety of types of inns was caused by the wide range in clientele—representatives of the British Government, public officials from adjoining colonies, travelers, both European and American, wealthy land owners and prospective buyers of land. In addition to these there were the middle class emigrants who were journeying into a new land, the sailors and others connected with the shipping interests, and the single merchants and professional men of the city, all who desired lodging.

Neither the "House for Strangers" nor one of similar standing could handle such a conglomerate, therefore it was necessary to have inns and taverns of varying qualities, so that each visitor might select a satisfactory stopping place.

The great number of establishments that existed in the Southern cities, particularly Savannah, before 1830, may be accounted for in several ways. Firstly, there were those innkeepers who were interested in following the tide of westward emigration. As new towns sprang into existence these people would open taverns, make a profit off the first comers and then remove to other localities. Secondly, there were those that became innkeepers thinking that they might be assisted to overcome a financial situation. This

[5] Hugh Finlay, *Journal kept by Hugh Finlay during his survey of the Post Offices between Falmouth . . . and Savannah in Georgia*, p. 60.
[6] Lee and Agnew, *op. cit.*, p. 10.

Old Stage Coach with mail compartment and six-horse covered wagon stopping at a typical inn of early days. From a sketch in possession of the National Museum, Washington, D. C. (Date unknown)

group would either prosper and then return to their previous occupations having accomplished the desired results, or they would fail in this as they had in former interests. Thirdly, many of the taverns, in the natural advance of business, changed hands every year or so, each time a new name being selected, thus giving the impression of many more taverns than actually existed. Many of the changes can be traced and have been noted in the "List of Taverns."[7]

While this was especially true in Savannah, a similar situation existed in Augusta, Mobile, and, in fact, in all of the settled communities, each section having its transient population that needed accommodation.

On the highways that connected these settlements, there were to be found inns and taverns of every description. Some were places where a traveler might find merely lodging for the night without conveniences, while others attempted to offer all that could be expected at a larger establishment in the city. The majority of the rural taverns were a day's journey apart, for no one cared to journey far after nightfall as the roads were too uncertain.

An interested person speaking of the conditions between Natchez and New Orleans, stated that travelers naturally preferred the "easy and comfortable mode of conveyance by steamboat to land journeys, rendered disagreeable by wretchedness of the roads, and still worse condition of the ... inns."[8]

In the South, therefore, at this time there existed every type of house of entertainment from the lowly hovel of the Indian to the finest the country could afford, in New Orleans. It would be well to note some specific examples, enough to give an adequate picture of the times. An old and experienced traveler, in the year 1783, wrote a letter to

[7] *See* appendix II.
[8] *Americans As They Are*, p. 142.

his daughter, who was about to open an inn, giving her the advice that he deemed necessary for the proper management of such an establishment.

Home, July, 1783.

Dear Bess—Entering on a new sphere of business, you will need advice. I am an old traveller, and know how to give it. The following remarks regard your treatment of genteel company: others will not expect such attention:

1. Let your house be kept neat. Have your furniture and rooms brushed and wiped every morning.
2. Keep scrapers at the outside doors, and mats at every door.
3. Let your bedsteads be cleansed every March, and you will be seldom troubled with multipedes, if you should be, use quicksilver and tallow.
4. Have your cooking done free from coals and ashes: frequently let your ham and chickens be broiled instead of fried.
5. Travellers like strong coffee, and well settled: but they cannot endure smoky or greasy tea.
6. Let your water bucket stand so high that your children shall not dabble in it.
7. Keep a spit box in each room: this will teach vulger persons that the floors were not made to spit on.
8. In a large establishment you may have two or three large rooms with several beds: but as a general thing, have small rooms and single.
9. Teach all around you to perform their duty in a silent manner; let each know the particular ring of the bell for him.
10. Let it be the business of one to receive strangers, and show them the common entrance room.
11. Don't allow your children to examine the baggage of your guests: nor to belch up wind at the table.
12. If you are intent on keeping a still, genteel house, noisy, vulger people will soon take the hint, and leave your worthy guests.
13. Furnish your public room with some good books, geographical and descriptive works, and papers for the season.

14. If you clear expenses the first season, you should be satisfied; for I am certain, unless you have greatly changed for the worse, since you left my roof, your winning manners will secure the return of old guests, and each will bring a new one for the next year.

If you follow the above directions and such suggestions, as will naturally arise in your inquisitive mind, your guests will always leave you with regret, and hasten to return to your well-managed establishment.

Your loving Father
Joshua Clifford.[9]

If inns and taverns had been managed according to these instructions, conditions would have been of higher standard, and travelers would not have found it necessary to describe the wretched conditions that prevailed in many of the frontier inns.

In one of the small hotels in Georgia there occurred an incident that bears repeating. A traveler after having spent the night in a little wayside inn was awakened at five o'clock in the morning by someone knocking violently at his door. Jumping up he ran to the door, calling out, 'What is the matter? What on earth do you want disturbing one at such an unreasonable hour in the morning?' 'Only want your sheets, sir.' 'My sheet! What do you want with my sheets?' 'Why sir, I want the sheets off your bed!' 'But what do you want them for?' To his astonishment the man replied, 'It is time to lay the table for breakfast, and I want your sheets to put on the tables, because they are the cleanest!' The gentleman thought if the sheets were to take the place of table-cloths, he would prefer his own to any other person's, and therefore allowed the man to come in and take them. When he made his appearance at breakfast, he was disgusted, but could not help being at the same time amused, to see so many persons innocently breakfasting off the supposed table-cloth.[10]

[9] Adiel Sherwood, *Gazetteer of the State of Georgia (1837)*, p. 46.
[10] Jane M. C. and Marion Turnbull, *American Photographs*, II, 77, 78; given in abbreviated form in *Louisville Daily Focus* I (1831), no. 84.

Not to leave the wrong impression the author continued by saying that "our readers must not ... suppose that such occurrences are common in the United States, for generally speaking they [the inns] are very clean."[11] This experience brings a similar one to mind that occurred in southern Georgia, the land of sand hills and wire grass, where lived some of the most abject of all the "poor white trash." Into the section came a professor and several students from the University of Georgia.

He stopped one evening at a small cabin to seek shelter for the night. The woman who met them at the door refused for a time to take them in on the plea that her husband was absent and she was unwilling to take in strangers. But she was assured that they would be content to take the fare she was able to give them, without putting her to extra trouble, provided they could find shelter for themselves and horses. There was only one room to the house and the woman was compelled, therefore, to stretch a sheet across a corner of the room behind which she put down a pallet for the men. In the preparation of the supper she used but one cooking utensil, and that a frying-pan, for cooking the meat, then the bread and afterward the coffee. When they had eaten their supper and the gentlemen had smoked their pipes, the woman warmed some water in the frying-pan and asked the travellers if they wished to wash their feet before retiring; but they declining, she remarked that she could not rest well without bathing her feet, and began immediately to wash them in the pan to the great horror and disgust of the gentlemen. This revelation was quite unpleasant to them and the next morning they breakfasted only on roasted potatoes and water.[12]

Featherstonhough gave an interesting picture of a tavern in Columbus, Georgia. After arriving in the town he and his party had gone out to see the falls of the Chattahoo-

[11] Turnbull, *op. cit.*
[12] P. H. Mell, *Life of Patrick Hues Mell*, pp. 126, 127.

chee, which were about a mile above the town. On their return they said that

> we endeavored to get something to eat, and were told to wait until the supper-bell rang; which having done with great patience, we moved, as soon as the tumultuous rush common on such occasions was effected, to the supper-table; and it was so full that it was quite impossible to get a seat there, neither was there another chair or bench in the room; so, knowing it would serve no purpose to show any impatience, we remained standing and looking on. The art of bolting was practiced here with as much success as I had seen it done at any other place, and in less than ten minutes every man without exception had gone back again to the bar-room; a circumstance that would have given us unalloyed pleasure, if they had not taken every scrap that had been set on the table along with them. We now made our wants known: and the mistress of the house learning that we were the two 'Men' that had come from the 'nation' in a carriage, very obligingly ordered some food to be produced for us, which, after a little more patience, we had the satisfaction of eating alone.[13]

Each courthouse town had one or more taverns, which did their most profitable business when court was in session. That week was always looked forward to with great delight.

> Every preparation was made for the judge and lawyers. Beds were aired and the bugs burned out. . . . The room usually appropriated to the Bench and the Bar was a great vagabond hall, denominated the barroom, and for this purpose appropriated once or twice a year. Along the bare walls of this mighty dormitory were arranged beds, each usually occupied by a couple of the limbs of the law, and sometimes appropriated to three. If there was not a spare apartment a bed was provided here for the Judge. And if there were no lawyers from Augusta, this one

[13] *Op. cit.*, II, 318-21.

was distinguished by the greatest mountain of feathers in the house.[14]

In Covington, the county seat of Newton County, Georgia, there was a tavern of unusual design. It was a log cabin designated in some parts of Georgia at that time, as a two-storied house, with both stories on the ground; in other words, a double penned cabin with a passage between. Uncle Ned, 'the proprietor,' had made ample provisions for the Bench and Bar. One pen of his house was appropriated to their use. There was a bed in each corner. . . . The interstices between the cabin poles were open, but there was no window and but one door, which had to be closed to avoid too close companionship with the dogs of the household. . . . In the center there stood a deal table of respectable dimensions, and this served the double purpose of dining-table and bed-place for one.[15]

Over in the Creek country at Fort Bainbridge there was a tavern kept by a Mrs. Harris, whose husband was headwaiter. Their inn was known to be the best in that country. "By special request, travelers might have private towels, and even a basin of water in their own rooms, instead of using the basin and roller towel in the hall. They might even have rooms with single beds. Guests without privileges, however, were expected to shave in the hall."[16]

It was at one of the Indian taverns in the Creek country, that a traveler, in 1833, after passing over the difficult roads, said that he stopped to change horses and procure supper. He told of his visit by saying, "We were now beyond the region of bread, and our fare consisted of eggs, broiled venison, and cakes of Indian corn fried in some kind of oleaginous matter."[17]

[14] John Donald Wade, *Augustus Baldwin Longstreet*, pp. 77, 78, quoted from William Henry Sparks, *The Memories of Fifty Years*, pp. 482-85.
[15] Wade, *op. cit.*, p. 79, quoted from Sparks, *op. cit.*, pp. 482-85.
[16] Lathrop, *op. cit.*, p. 230.
[17] *Men and Manners in America*, I, 129-32.

Despite criticisms by travelers of the inns throughout the South, these same taverns filled an important need in the community. It was usually within their walls that the early patriots met and laid their plans for action. There was one tavern in Savannah that was particularly noted for such meetings. The first liberty pole that was raised in Georgia was raised in front of Tondee's Tavern on June 5, 1775, the birthday of His Majesty King George III, and on July 4, the Provincial Congress met in the Long Room of the Tavern.[18]

The inns and taverns of the eighteenth century were, as are our hotels of the twentieth century, "the centre of life and affairs for the men folk; and judges and jurymen, church committees and politicians, idlers and business men, all resorted thither, to discuss and arrange affairs together."[19] The Cincinnati, the Union Society, and numerous other organizations used the inns as places to hold their regular meetings.

It is interesting to read the advertisements that appeared in the papers. The following are typical examples, chosen at random from the mass of newspaper advertisements.

EAGLE TAVERN

The subscriber has taken the establishment formerly occupied by Col. Geo. Fisher, and he hopes by unremitted attention to the wants and conveniences of boarders and travellers, to obtain a liberal share of patronage.

His table will be furnished with every luxury the country and market afford. His rooms are convenient and airy; gentlemen with families, or private parties can be furnished with private apartments.

His stable is well furnished and faithful and experienced ostlers will always attend. Josiah Everitt.[20]

---

[18] Lee and Agnew, *op. cit.*, pp. 35, 37.
[19] James Schouler, *Americans of 1776*, p. 77.
[20] *The Floridian* (Tallahassee), I (1828), No. 7, which is included as a supplement to J. O. Knauss, *Territorial Florida Journalism*.

DANIEL OCAIN IN SAVANNAH

Hath opened a house of entertainment to board or lodge any persons that please to favour him with their custom. He hath a large and good assortment of liquors, also food for men and horses, and will charge as low a price as possible; good usage and cash payments shall balance each other; and constant attention shall be given by

Daniel Ocain

Who continues to make and mend all sorts of saddles and horse furniture, at his house near the Hon. James Habersham, Esq's in Johnson Square.[21]

TO THE PUBLICK

The Subscriber, at the request of his friends, will, on Monday next, the 16th instant, open A HOTEL, on the Bay of Savannah, in the house lately occupied by Mr. Flint, to be known by the name of the

STATE HOTEL

He has, at a great expense, procured the best liquors of every kind. As he is determined to open the Hotel for the reception of Gentlemen (only), it will be conducted in that style which will give general satisfaction, do credit to the state and the Publick's humble servant

Jan. 10, 1786

Wm. Thompson[22]

THE SAVANNAH COFFEE HOUSE

Lately opened on the Bay, is now completely furnished. The situation needs no recommendation, as it is delightfully pleasant, and the house elegant and convenient. There is a most spacious dining-room, where almost any number can be provided with a dinner on a short notice; it is also very convenient for a Dancing Assembly or private Balls: Likewise a number of private rooms, where gentlemen may meet to transact business; or for their amusement: There are also several pleasant lodging rooms with fireplaces, where boarders or lodgers can be retired almost as in

---

[21] *Georgia Gazette,* 1766, No. 144.
[22] *Gazette of the State of Georgia,* 1786, No. 155, 156, 157, 158, 159.

a private family. Coffee is furnished at any minute from seven in the morning to nine at night. Gentlemen can be provided with breakfast, dinner, supper or lodging. A book of intelligence is kept, from which information may be had of all vessels entering or clearing out of the port of Savannah, passengers names, and occurrences. All the principal newspapers will be procured from the different states of the union.

The subscriber will always endeavor to procure the first qualities from the cellar and stall, and hope and flatter themselves that, from the strict attention they shall pay to the business and the punctual attention they will give, to merit the approbation of those who may be so kind as to favour them with their custom. Savannah November 17, 1785   Burt and Stebbins.[23]

CITY HOTEL

run by Edward Byrd and James R. Danforth

The Northern, Charleston and Milledgeville stages stop at the City Hotel, where their respective offices are kept.[24]

In New Orleans during the first half of the nineteenth century, there were built many hotels and taverns that well deserved the name. Beside these there were the smaller and cruder inns that were so common in all parts of the South. The smaller ones were all alike no matter where they were located. As a traveler remarked in regard to those of New Orleans, "Their tap is eternally going. Do the police ever intrude? Mine host finds a ready argument to calm his suspicions; the privileged villain tips the officer a piece of silver or gold, according to his rank."[25] The major part of the income of the tavern-keeper was from his liquor, and he prided himself in his selection; but he also operated an ordinary, in which food could be obtained, and maintained rooms for lodging. There were French inns and American inns, each catering to its own group.

[23] *Gazette of the State of Georgia*, 1785, No. 147.
[24] *Georgia Advertiser* (Augusta), III (1821), No. 259.
[25] Berquin-Duvallon, *op. cit.*, pp. 54, 55.

Beside these rather insignificant taverns, there were the elaborate hotels. These were merely a development of the inn or tavern to meet the needs and desires of a more aristocratic clientele. There were several that were prominent and should be described, for they stood out in high relief against the drab background.

The Exchange Hotel, according to an old City Directory of New Orleans, was a "truly magnificent establishment, which for size and architectural beauty, stands unrivalled."[26]

It was commenced in the summer of 1835, by an incorporated company. The building was designed by, and erected, under the superintendance of J. Gallier, architect, and cost six hundred thousand dollars, including the ground on which it stands, which cost one hundred thousand dollars. It presents a front on each of three streets, the principal one on St. Charles Street, consisting of a projecting portico of six Corinthian columns, which stands upon a granite basement fourteen feet high, with a pediment on the top, and four similar columns on each side of the portico, placed in a range with the front wall: behind which is formed a recess fifteen feet wide, and one hundred and thirty-nine feet long, and floored over with large granite slabs, which, supported on iron beams, serve for a ceiling to that portion of the basement story standing under the portico; and on top a delightful promenade under the shade of the portico and side columns. From this platform, by a range of marble steps, is the entrance to the saloon. The entrance to the barroom is under the portico; and the outside steps leading from the street to the portico, are placed on each side thereof between it and the front range of the building. In one of the rear angles of the building is a bathing establishment, consisting of fourteen rooms elegantly fitted up with every convenience for hot or cold bathing; on the opposite angle are placed the wine cellars, storehouse, fuel-house, &c. all the remaining parts of the basement are divided into stores, which are rented out to various trades-

[26] B. M. Norman, *Norman's New Orleans and Environs*, pp. 137-41, illustration, p. 138.

people. The bar-room is in the basement rear of the centre of the edifice and is octagonal in the plan, seventy feet in diameter and twenty feet high, having an interior range of Ionic columns, distributed so as to support the weight of the floors and partitions of the upper stories. The architecture of this room is Ionic, and that of the saloon, which is immediately above the ball-room is of the Corinthian order, and eighteen feet high. . . .

A grand spiral staircase commences upon the centre of the saloon floor, and is continued up to the dome; around this staircase, on each side of the upper stories, is formed a gallery, which gives access to six bed rooms within the octagon on each of the six upper stories. The whole arrangement of the octagon is very original and very ingenious, and the convenient manner in which the passages and stairs are contrived to communicate with the adjoining wings of the building, is deserving of much praise. As the bar-room is six feet higher than the other parts of the basement, the entrance to the saloon from the portico is by a flight of marble steps, twelve in number, and thirty-five feet long; on the top of the marble steps is placed a beautiful marble statue of Washington, procured in Italy.

The gentlemen's dining and sitting rooms occupy the whole side of the building on Gravier Street. The dining-room, with a pantry at the end; is one hundred and twenty-nine feet long by fifty wide, and twenty-two feet high, tastefully finished in the Corinthian order with two inside ranges of columns, so placed that there is abundant space for ranges of tables, sufficient to accommodate five hundred persons. The ladies' dining-room is placed over the bathing apartments and is fifty-two by thirty-six feet. The kitchen, fifty-eight by twenty-nine feet, is placed in the rear wing of the building, on the same story with, and in the centre between the dining rooms. The two angles of the principal front contains the ladies' drawing room, and the men's sitting room, the former forty by thirty-two feet, the latter thirty-eight feet square. . . . There are nine private parlors on the second story, to some of which are attached adjoining bedrooms, and the same number on the upper stories. There are four stories of elegantly furnished and well-lighted bed-rooms all around the four sides of the building, with central passages or corridors which communicate with the centre and with each other having three stairs opening to the corridors, besides the grand stair-case in the octagon. There are, in the edifice, three hundred and fifty rooms.

A dome, of beautiful proportions, after a plan of Dakin, forty-six feet in diameter, surmounts the octagon building, elevated upon an order of fluted columns, which stand eleven feet from the dome, around the outside, and on the dome is elevated an elegant little Corinthian turret. There is a large circular room under the dome, on the floor of which the circular colonade forms a beautiful gallery eleven feet wide, from whence can be seen the whole city, and all the windings of the river for several miles in each direction. The effect of the dome upon the sight of the visitor, as he approaches the city, is similar to that of St. Paul's, London.

No better evidence can be adduced—nor more flattering encomiums presented to the architect, than the fact of the indescribable effect of the sublime and matchless proportions of this building upon all spectators—even the stoical Indian and the cold and strange backwoodsman, when they first view it, are struck with wonder and delight. The view of this structure by moonlight is a sight not easily described. The furnishings of this establishment cost $150,000.00.[27]

The dimensions of the hotel are very impressive when arranged in tabular form.

Length along the principal front	235 feet
Length on Gravier Street	195 feet
Length on Common Street	160 feet
Height from ground to top of general cornice	75 feet
Height to top of upper tower	185 feet
Height to top of dome	160 feet
Height to circular colonade under dome	96 feet
Height to top of cornice over colonade	126 feet

[27] Norman, *op. cit.*, pp. 137-41, illustration, p. 138.

Height to top of flagg staff.........................203 feet
Number of rooms ....350[28]

Another hotel was situated diagonally opposite the Exchange at the corner of St. Charles and Common Streets. This edifice was known as the Verandah, since it had a projecting roof and balcony across the front, which protected not only the guests of the hotel but also the pedestrians from the sun and rain.

The city directory of New Orleans for the year 1842 declared that the Verandah, which was begun in October, 1836,

is destined as a family hotel by its enterprising projector and builder, B. O. Pritchard Esq.—It was finished in May, 1838. . . . The great dining room, is, probably, one of the highest finished apartments in America. The ceiling, especially, is a model; being composed of three beautiful elliptic domes for chandeliers—dimensions of this room 85 feet by 32, and 27 feet high. The chimney pieces of the parlors are fine pieces of sculpture, and the rooms are likewise handsome. A statue of Venus adorns the ladies' private entrance, on St. Charles Street. The cost of the edifice, land, &c., was $300,000. The whole was designed, and has been constructed by Messrs. Dakin & Dakin, architects, well known in the city.[29]

The hotels, inns, and boarding-houses were numerous and quite varied, including the strictly French ones that catered to the foreign trade and to the Americans who desired French food. The American hotels were more cosmopolitan and consequently had the larger clientele. In Appendix II many of these establishments are listed according to their respective localities and approximate dates of founding. Many of these taverns have been forgotten, the only

[28] *New Orleans Directory for 1842*, p. 67.
[29] *Ibid.*, pp. 67, 68; Norman, *op. cit.*, pp. 141, 142, illustration p. 142; *New Orleans Directory for 1838*, illustration opp. p. 332.

existing record being a chance mention in a travel journal or diary of that period. A more complete description would be desired but in most cases cannot be had. The average traveler did not consider the inn or tavern worthy of many words, mentioning only that he spent the night at the establishment of a Mr. Smith or whatever the name might have been.

Another phase that is worthy of note in a discussion of inns is that of the charges for accommodations and services. The tariff varied according to the place and period. J. F. D. Smyth, during his tour of the South in 1784, gave the following schedule of charges:

Dinner	1 shilling
Supper	1 shilling
Breakfast	8 pence
Servant's diet	6 pence if they are black, but for white servants you pay the same as for yourself
Lodging	4 pence
Stabling for your horse	6 pence each besides paying for their provender; Indian corn, or more generally rough rice, with which horses are fed, two pence per quart.[30]

In 1820 a hotel in Huntsville, Alabama, advertised its rates as follows:

Breakfast	37½c
Dinner	50c
Supper	37½c
Horse for the night	50c
Lodging	12½c
Boarding without lodging, per week	$3.50

[30] Smyth, *op. cit.*, II, 39.

Boarding with lodging, per week...................... 4.50
Horse, per week .... 3.00[81]

Other lists of charges are available, but these are typical and represent the average charges made.

The type of hotel or tavern established in a community was an index to the degree of refinement that was prevalent in the locality. As a rule, frontier conditions carried with them their component parts, crude log taverns, inadequate roads, and undesirable living quarters. As these conditions passed, more stable communities came into existence. The desire and hope for permanence spurred the inhabitants to build more substantial and comfortable buildings and to improve conditions of travel and transportation.

[81] (Huntsville) *Alabama Republican*, Nov. 17, 1820, quoted in E. C. Betts, *Early History of Huntsville, Alabama*, p. 76.

CHAPTER VII
IMPROVEMENTS IN TRANSPORTATION

THE ROADS of a community or a country are accurate and positive indications of the degree of its civilization.

Roads are the veins and arteries of the body politic, for through them flow the agricultural productions and the commercial supplies which are the life-blood of the state. Upon the sufficiency of their number, the propriety of their directions, and the unobstructedness of their courses, depend the ease and the rapidity with which the more distant portions of the system receive the nutriment which is essential to their life, health, and vigor, and without a copious supply of which the extremities must languish and die.[1]

It has been pointed out in the previous chapters that the condition of the roads in the Old South was deplorable. Traffic moved slowly and was very uncertain. It was the desire of everyone to see something done that would eradicate these deficiencies. In 1818, Governor William W. Bibb, in a message to the Legislative Council and House of Representatives of Alabama, voiced the sentiment of the progressive South. "Permit me to recommend to the attention of the legislature the subject of roads, ferries, and bridges. The strength of the country consists in its population and it is peculiarly the interest of this territory to invite emigrants hither, by furnishing every possible facility of communication."[2] Within a few years funds were placed at the disposal of the General Assembly for the construction of roads. It was hoped that this would make possible the establishment of good highways throughout the state. The

[1] W. M. Gillespie, *Manual of Road-Making*, p. 15.
[2] *Niles' Weekly Register*, XIV (1818), 44.

merchant, the planter, and the traveler were all interested in the project.[3]

With the improved conditions in the section of the United States south of the Appalachian Mountains came an increase in immigration. It is therefore necessary, in order to understand this phase of westward movement, to discuss a few of the improvements of roads. There are three general topics to be taken into consideration: first, bridges; second, ferries; and third, roads.

Mention has already been made in Chapter I of the bridges constructed by the Indians. The early trails usually followed the banks and streams, making detours to avoid low bottoms and swamps.[4] Smaller branches and creeks were crossed by fords when shallow; and when too deep to be waded, they were crossed by means of a "raccoon bridge,"[5] which was a tree trunk felled to reach from bank to bank. When the Spaniards came to this country, in the beginning of the sixteenth century, they found this type of bridge in existence. The European usually had to have one more substantially constructed as he was not agile in crossing on the rounded surface of a log. Bartram in 1777 mentioned a "raccoon bridge" saying, "over this my Indian friend would trip with one hundred weight of leather on his back, as quick and light as that quadruped, when I was scarcely able to shuffle myself over it astride."[6] The log bridges were not permanent structures; they were never built with a thought of the future but rather as a momentary convenience. In the early period there was no need of a bridge that would endure, as the traveler did not contemplate retracing his steps. With the stream of immigration becoming more firmly fixed in certain, regular channels

[3] *Mobile Argus,* I (1823), November 4.
[4] Cf. Sergeant, *op. cit.,* p. 65.
[5] Henry E. Chambers, *Mississippi Valley Beginnings,* p. 13.
[6] Peter A. Brannon, *Highway Boats and Bridges,* pp. 18, 19.

and not so diversified as previously, the need for permanent, stable bridges presented itself.

Contemporary accounts are filled with the experiences of travelers as they encountered the bridges of this transitory period; that is, the period before the permanent bridge. One remarked that, "Even by daylight our way was beset by difficulties. First came Killbeedy Creek, which we crossed by as awkward and rickety a bridge as can well be imagined. Then came Persimmon's swamp, which presented a delightful corduroy road, some parts of which had been entirely absorbed by the morass."[7] When the streams were flooded the condition was even worse. Latrobe said that he would rather have taken his chances and swum the streams "than pass the rocking and fearful erections which, under that name [bridge], span many of the deep rivers on the roads nearer the coast, and however rotten, are seldom repaired till some fatal accident renders the repair imperative."[8] Latrobe continued by describing one of the structures:

The 'bad bridge' over a powerful stream was said to have been carried from its position by the flood, and to be totally impassable. This after getting within fifty miles of Tallahassee, seemed too provoking, but we had got over many 'impassable' places before, by a process amounting to carrying the 'carry-all,' and we hoped to do so again. In fact the danger diminished as we advanced, and the vehicle, lightened as far as was practicable, was conducted safely through the water upon the disjointed and submerged bridge, while Portales and myself waded with all humility after, with the chance of a bite from an old alligator.[9]

Featherstonhough described a similar instance in a different locality:

[7] Thomas Hamilton, *op. cit.*, p. 374.
[8] Charles Joseph Latrobe, *The Rambler in North America*, II, 64.
[9] *Ibid.*, p. 50.

IMPROVEMENTS IN TRANSPORTATION 119

On reaching the Kateebee swamp we found the bridge of logs, which extended about a mile, quite dislocated with the incessant passage of waggons and the rise of the waters. A file of them had just passed it with great difficulty, and on taking a look at the numerous holes made in it, some of which were four feet deep, I despaired of getting our vehicle over. . . . Almost the whole of one bridge was under water and in one part of it, the structure had been quite broken up for a distance of at least 200 yards, the horse treading fearfully amongst the logs, some of which were floating and some sticking in the mud, not a little puzzled how to get out of these chasms. . . .[10]

It would seem that all bridges were constructed in an unsatisfactory manner, and these conditions were not and could not be improved until a means of financing the structures was employed. The toll bridge met just such a need. While not a new institution in the South, much less in the United States, its reception in the Southern states was not immediate nor by any means universal. Its adoption, however, usually meant improved conditions as far as bridges were concerned. Northern Florida had several bridges that had permits from the state to charge toll.[11] Governor Claiborne was interested in seeing a toll bridge established over a bayou near New Orleans.[12] Toll bridges were built over the larger rivers such as the Savannah at Augusta[13] and the Chattahoochee at Columbus.[14]

The bridge at Augusta was outstanding in history.

In 1790 the ferry franchise of 1768 was lodged by the legislature of Georgia in Wade Hampton, of South Carolina, with the further right to build a bridge over the river at or near the ferry site. The bridge was to be at least sixteen feet in width, and, as a rent therefor, Hampton was annually to pay to the com-

[10] *Excursion through the Slave States*, II, 313.
[11] Caroline Mays Brevard, *History of Florida*, I, 174.
[12] *Official Letter Books of W. C. C. Claiborne*, V, 136, 137.
[13] John Pope, *A Tour through the Southern and Western Territories*, p. 74.
[14] *Columbus, Georgia, 1827-1865* (pt. I), p. 32.

missioners of Augusta fifty pounds sterling, securing such rental by a mortgage of the bridge and one acre of land on the South Carolina side, on which the land abutted.[15]

The bridge was ready for use February 17, 1791, and the following was the authorized schedule of charges:

master, professors and all students, for the
time being, of Richmond Academy.......gratis
foot passengers ....3 pence
man on horseback ....6 pence
four horse wagon, loaded................4 shillings, 8 pence[16]

On May 21, 1791, George Washington, on his tour through the South passed over this bridge.[17] In July of that year John Pope was visiting in Augusta and commented on conditions there, saying that "A wonderful Spirit for Building seems to have permeated this place— A fine elegant Bridge of superior strength to any of its Size I ever saw, stretches itself over the noble River Savannah, right abreast of the Town, where it is navigable for vessels of 50 or 60 Tons Burthen."[18]

In 1796 the bridge was swept away by the "Yazoo Freshet" and in the next year the state legislature renewed Hampton's grant and gave him two years from that date to replace the structure.[19] It was completed in 1799 but suffered the same fate as the previous one. In 1809 the state legislature empowered Walter Leigh and Edward Rowell to construct another bridge and fixed the schedule of tolls as follows:

foot passengers ....$ .06¼
hogshead of tobacco .... .25
four horse wagon loaded................................ 1.00[20]

[15] Charles Colcock Jones, Jr., *Memorial History of Augusta, Georgia*, p. 477.
[16] *Ibid.*
[17] *Diaries of George Washington*, IV, 181. [18] Pope, *op. cit.*, p. 74.
[19] Jones, *Memorial History of Augusta, Georgia*, p. 477.
[20] *Ibid.*

Henry Ker in his travels through the section in 1816, mentioned that he crossed this structure.[21]

The following may be considered a typical example of rates charged by toll bridges during this period:

man and horse ....4 pence
carriage, drawn by one or two horses or oxen.........1 shilling
horse, mare, or oxen, each...........................4 pence
head of neat cattle, each............................1 penny
20 hogs or sheep and in proportion for a greater or
    lesser number of hogs or sheep..................1 shilling[22]

One difficulty that was encountered when roads were opened through the Indian country was that the cattle and horses of the Indians would wander too far from home. In order to prevent this it was decided that gates be erected on the bridges; thus the animals could not stray any great distance.[23]

Another improvement was the introduction of the ferry. Travelers could then be reasonably sure of having a means of crossing the larger streams. One of the earliest provisions relative to ferries was mentioned in the *Colonial Records of Georgia* for the year 1735. According to this statement "there are forty men appointed to clear a path from Barnwell's Bluff (north side of Altamaha River—South Settlement) to Savannah, and Mr Oglethorpe designs, that every six miles shall be a Village, and that at every River there shall be another with a Ferry Boat."[24]

The establishment and maintenance of ferries was expensive, and for this reason it was considered reasonable that the people living in the immediate vicinity of the road or ferry should bear a part of the cost. This was the view held

---
[21] *Travels through the Western Interior of the United States*, p. 345.
[22] *North Carolina State Records*, XXIII, 368.
[23] *American State Papers, Indian Affairs*, I, 650; also Document No. 92, 7th Congress, 1st Session.
[24] *Colonial Records of Georgia*, XXI, 115.

by an officer of the Colony of Georgia in a communication addressed to Benjamin Martyn.

> It is certain, Sir, that good roads are of the greatest benefit to any country . . . but we think, if they mean the Trustees to make them wholly, that they have asked a Favour, which must create a monstrous expense—if indeed their Honours shou'd be pleased to be at the expense of Ferry Boats to cross certain Rivers, or of making Bridges over some Creeks, we think it wou'd be highly reasonable, that the Inhabitants should be obliged by a law made for that purpose to make Roads, as in other colonies. . . .[25]

Thus in 1750-51 opinion was being formulated especially in Georgia with the purpose of having the inhabitants participate in a program of improving transportation facilities.

In 1755 an act was passed defining the duties of the surveyors in the Province of Georgia. One of the duties assigned was that they might establish ferries where they deemed it necessary and procure proper boats and persons to attend them. It was also their responsibility to decide the fares to be charged.[26] With this enactment the major responsibility was placed in the hands of the surveyors named in the act, "An act to empower the several Surveyors hereafter named to lay out Public Roads in the Province of Georgia."[27] Other ferries than those established by the group of men were authorized after a bill had been submitted to, considered by, and acted upon by the Council. The ferry established over the Great Ogechee River at the place called Pine Bluff was a typical example. On May 8, 1761, the bill was presented and read for the first time.[28] The bill called for the establishing of "a Ferry over Great Ogechee River at the Place called Pine Bluff and Vesting the same in John Deveaux Esqr. His Executors and administra-

[25] *Ibid.*, XXVI, 167, 168. [27] *Ibid.*, pp. 88-92.
[26] *Ibid.*, XVIII, 100. [28] *Ibid.*, XIII, 547.

IMPROVEMENTS IN TRANSPORTATION

tors for the Space of Seven years."[29] It was read the second time,[30] and finally approved by the Governor.[31] On January 19, 1762, Joseph Wright petitioned for the privilege of operating this ferry at Pine Bluff since John Deveaux had died.[32]

In 1765 there was a ferry across the Savannah River connecting the Parish of St. Paul with Fort Augusta, in South Carolina.[33] On March 6, 1766, a ferry was established across the Savannah from the plantation of Miles Brewton to Rochester in South Carolina.[34] According to the agreement there was to be kept one or more ferry boats, of sufficient size to carry six horses. Also there would be kept one white man and a sufficient number of slaves or servants to attend the ferry boat night and day.[35] Any delay would cost the operator at least fifteen shillings per hour.[36] The charges made were as follows:

1 foot traveller	1 shilling
each person and horse	3 shillings
wheel carriage	9 pennies per wheel
single horse	1 shilling, 6 pennies
neat cattle	1 shilling, 6 pennies, per head
calves, sheep, hogs	4 pennies per head

exceptions
  Governor
  Commander in Chief
  all messengers sent in service of State
  postmen, themselves, horses, carriages, servants, baggage[37]

In 1768 a ferry was established by the Colonial Government from the center of Augusta to the opposite bluff on the

---

[29] *Ibid.*, XIX (pt. I), 60.
[30] *Ibid.*, XIII, 550.
[31] *Ibid.*, p. 582.
[32] *Ibid.*, p. 639.
[33] *Ibid.*, XIV, 216.
[34] *Ibid.*, XVIII, 764.
[35] *Ibid.*, p. 766.
[36] *Ibid.*, p. 767.
[37] *Ibid.*, pp. 766, 767.

Carolina shore of the Savannah River.[88] Several other ferries were established by the act; namely, "a ferry over the river Altamaha at Fort Barrington,"[39] "a public ferry ... from the town of Ebenezer upon the Savannah river to the Bluff on the opposite shore,"[40] and "two Ferrys over Brian Creek, one at a place called Mill-Town and the other at the upper Public Road."[41] The ferries designated in this act were to be in operation for five years from the passing of the act.[42] The requirements for these ferries were the same as for the one previously mentioned at Pine Bluff.

The schedule of charges as designated by the act was as follows:

	Augusta[43]	Ebenezer[44]	BrianCreek either ferry[45]
foot passenger	2 pence	2 pence	1 penny
person and horse	4 pence	6 pence	3 pence
wheel carriage, per wheel	2 pence	3 pence	1½ penny
single horse	2 pence	3 pence	1½ penny
single horse, if swam	1 penny	1½ penny	
neat cattle, per head	2 pence	3 pence	1½ penny
neat cattle, if swam, per head	1½ penny	1½ penny	1 penny
calves, sheep, hogs, per head	1 penny	1 penny	½ penny
calves, sheep, hogs, if swam, per head	½ penny	½ penny	½ penny

Fort Barrington—

	if to the opposite shore[46]	to Mutteer's Landing[47] or from Santa Sevilia
foot passenger	2 pence	2 shillings

[88] Jones, *Memorial History of Augusta, Georgia*, p. 477.
[89] *Colonial Records of Georgia*, XIX (pt. I), 3.
[40] *Ibid.*
[41] *Ibid.*
[42] *Ibid.*, p. 4.
[43] *Ibid.*, p. 6.
[44] *Ibid.*, p. 5.
[45] *Ibid.*, p. 6.
[46] *Ibid.*, pp. 6, 7.
[47] *Ibid.*, p. 7.

person and horse	6 pence	4 shillings, 6 pence
wheel carriage, per wheel	3 pence	2 shillings, 3 pence
single horse	3 pence	2 shillings, 3 pence
single horse, if swam	1½ penny	
neat cattle, per head	3 pence	
neat cattle, if swam, per head	1½ penny	
calves, sheep, hogs, per head	1 penny	
calves, sheep, hogs, if swam, per head	½ penny	

The charges in the second column were only necessary, according to the act, when "there should be such a freshet in the River Altamaha as render it impracticable to go through the swamp on the opposite side; then and in that case it shall and may be Lawfull for the said Ferryman, to demand and receive 'these rates' for Ferriage to Mutteer's Landing and the same if brought from Santa Sevilia."[48]

The contract of 1761, for the operation of the ferry at Pine Bluff, had expired, and according to the act of 1768 the commissioners were authorized and empowered to put up for public sale, and "to sell the said Ferry and the rents, Issues, Profits, produce, and Ferriage of the same to the best bidder for the term of five years to Commence from the day of the sale."[49] The requirements stipulated were that "a good and sufficient Ferry Boat not less than nine feet wide and twenty feet long and a good Canoe with two or more white servants or two or more slaves for the purpose of transporting all Passengers, their carriages, Servants, horses, and cattle" should be continuously available.[50] The rates were:

foot passengers	2	pence
person and horse	6	pence

[48] *Ibid.*
[49] *Ibid.*, p. 60.   [50] *Ibid.*, p. 62.

wheel carriage, per wheel	3	pence
single horse, per head	3	pence
neat cattle, per head	3	pence
neat cattle, if swam, per head	1½	penny
calves, sheep, hogs, per head	1	penny
calves, sheep, hogs, if swam, per head	½	penny

"All which rates and Prices shall be paid and received from all persons and at all times except in times of Actual Service upon Alarms, Insurrections, or invasions when the Ferriage shall be free and also except his Majesties Troops upon duty and Ministers of the Gospel."[51]

When the lease on the Pine Bluff ferry expired in September 1773, it was to be leased again until December 31, 1773, and then put up for sale for five years. The equipment and charges remained the same as in 1768 with the single exception that the "students in Divinity of Bethesda" were to be allowed free passage.[52]

Hugh Finlay mentioned a ferry known as "Ashley ferry . . . 10 miles from Charles Town,"[53] which was well attended. The equipment here consisted of flats or skows, as they were locally known, which were drawn by means of a rope across the river, which was about thirty yards across. Another ferry of the same type was described by a traveler: "The coach was run into the ferryboat, and by means of a hawser stretched across the river, we soon found ourselves in safety on the opposite shore."[54]

Two ferries that were on the Savannah River during this period deserve notice. One of them was known as the "Three Sisters,"[55] which had a dining-room in connection with it; the other was the Middlesex Ferry, commonly called

---

[51] *Ibid.*, pp. 62, 63.
[52] *Ibid.*, p. 340.   [53] *Op. cit.*, p. 52.
[54] *Men and Manners in America*, I, 129.
[55] William Bartram, *Travels*, p. 307.

"Zubly's."[56] The conditions that existed here prior to 1785 must have been undesirable, for there appeared in the *Gazette of the State of Georgia* the following notice, to inform the public

> that the bridges and causeway leading to the ferry there are now mended, as well as they could be at this time, and that they have procured a flat, which is under the direction of John Grubb, living there; so that all persons may now pass with convenience. The owner is sorry the situation of the place, and of the times, render it necessary for the present to make the rate of ferriage a little higher than before the war. Mr. Grubb has expressed direction to keep no ferry books.[57]

Included in many of the Indian treaties promulgated during the opening years of the nineteenth century were statements similar to the one with the Chickasaws. After some discussion as to the rights of way through their nation, the treaty continued by stating "that the necessary ferries over the water courses crossed by the said road shall be held and deemed to be the property of the Chickasaw Nation."[58]

Berquin-Duvallon, while traveling in Louisiana, was impressed by the fact that there did not exist an easy means of communication from one bank of the Mississippi to the other. He continued by saying that

> No ferry boats cross over at regular prices; the chief obstacle along the river at its period of elevation. . . . This defect of communication, which is only partially obviated by canoes, will conduce to keep the right shore of the river . . . in a state less active and flourishing than the left. . . .[59]

Several other ferries located in the South, but which did not play any distinctive part in westward penetration, were

---
[56] *Gazette of the State of Georgia*, No. 136, 137 (1785).
[57] *Ibid.*
[58] *Indian Affairs, Laws and Treaties*, II, 55, 56.
[59] *Op. cit.*, pp. 17, 18.

Holt's Ferry,[60] across the Oconee River at Fort Wilkinson, Dale's Ferry,[61] on the Alabama River, Colbert's Ferry[62] located on the road between Natchez and Mobile, and a ferry which operated between Blakely and Mobile.[63]

The improvements made in connection with the bridges and ferries were the most outstanding advancements of this period. No other one improvement meant so much to the traveler as that which promised certitude of being able to cross the water courses in security and with reasonable rapidity. There was a movement on foot to improve the general conditions, as was mentioned in connection with the post-roads. Three forms of improvement may be mentioned in passing; first, the plank road; second, the corduroy road; and third, the shell road.

Gillespie in his *Manual of Road Making* had a description of the method of laying a plank road.

In the most generally approved system, two parallel rows of small sticks of timber (called indifferently sleepers, stringers, or sills) are embedded in the road, three or four feet apart. Planks, eight feet long, and three or four inches thick, are laid upon these sticks, across them, at right angles to their direction. A side track of earth, to turn out upon, is carefully graded. Deep ditches are dug at each side, to ensure perfect drainage; and thus is formed a Plank Road.[64]

Many people held great hopes for this method of road-making. In some localities they were called the "Farmer's Railroad" for he was the one that profited most by their construction, although all classes in the community were benefited. The peculiar merit of plank roads as given by Gil-

---

[60] *Georgia Journal*, I (1810), No. 41, II (1811), No. 2.
[61] *Niles' Weekly Register*, XIV (1818), 335.
[62] *American State Papers, Indian Affairs*, II, 80.
[63] *Niles' Weekly Register*, XXIV (1823), 294-95, quoted from *New York American*.
[64] P. 231; cf. p. 244.

Between New London and Lynchburg and 5½ miles from Lynchburg. From "Virginia Illustrated," by Porte Crayon, in *Harpers Magazine* for 1856.

lespie was "that the great diminution of friction upon them makes them more akin to railroads than to common roads, with the advantages over railroads, that everyone can drive his own wagon upon them."[65]

Another advocate of this type of road was William Gregg who wrote an *Essay on Plank Roads*. He remarked that among the great improvements which had so materially aided in diffusing the comforts of human life, the plank road was destined to occupy a prominent place. Continuing, he stated that "good common roads tend to change the condition of the farmer wherever they are extended; the plank-road gives him a thoroughfare infinitely superior to any other, not excepting the railroad."[66] It was not an entirely satisfactory type of road, but it was decidedly better than the existing dirt road with its attending mud.[67]

When a road passed over soft swampy ground, which was kept moist by springs and could not be drained without too great expense, it could be cheaply and rapidly made passable by constructing a "corduroy" road. The first step was to fell a sufficient number of young trees, as straight and as uniform as possible and then lay them side by side across the road. The spaces between the logs, which varied from the usual one or two inches to several inches, were filled with earth which was well rammed.[68] Gillespie made the remark:

though its successive hills and hollows offer great resistance to draught, and are very unpleasant to persons riding over it, it is never-the-less a very valuable substitute for a swamp, which in its natural state would at times be utterly impassable. But necessary and desirable as these roads may be to accomplish such an end in the infancy of a settlement, their retention upon a great

[65] *Ibid.*, p. 249.
[66] P. 3.
[67] *Florida Plantation Records*, p. 61.   [68] Gillespie, *op. cit.*, p. 228.

thoroughfare is a disgraceful proof of indolence and want of enterprise in those who habitually travel over them.[69]

The corduroy road received a great amount of ridicule, but it was far superior to the swamp land it traversed.

The shell road that extended from New Orleans to Carrollton on Lake Pontchartrain, a distance of six miles, was the only good road out of the Crescent City.[70] It was composed of oyster shells and aided greatly in the movement of traffic in and out of New Orleans.

Conditions relative to transportation in the South changed very slowly. James Stirling in a letter dated February 4, 1857, commented on conditions. He had been discussing tests of progress and concluded by saying that

another criterion of civilization is roads. Judged by its roads, the South is far behind. In Kentucky I saw some good roads. In Tennessee they have some 'pikes' (turnpike-roads), and some 'mud-roads'. In Louisiana, Alabama, and Georgia, I have as yet met no well-made road. In the town of Montgomery I saw a country wagon with six mules, and the spokes of the wheels were plastered up to the very naves with thick tenacious mud. And Montgomery is the capital of the State! Such deficiencies in Minnesota did not surprise me: that was yesterday but a forest; but Tennessee dates from 1796, Louisiana from 1812, and Georgia is one of the original thirteen. She, at least, might have got clear of 'mud-roads' in the sixty-eight years of her independence.[71]

[69] *Ibid.*
[70] Turnbull, *op. cit.*, pp. 56, 57; Norman, *op. cit.*, p. 192.
[71] *Letters from the Slave States*, pp. 179-80.

CHAPTER VIII
MODES OF CONVEYANCE

WHEN WHEELED vehicles began to pass over the widened trails, roads in the South in their true sense originated. The routes were straightened, unnecessary curves eliminated and stumps and trees cleared away. The resulting road was rough and difficult to travel, and only the most massive of vehicles could withstand the rocks and ruts that were ever present. "Although carts and wagons were often used in the Atlantic seaboard states before the Revolutionary period, they did not appear on roads between the Alleghenies and the Mississippi Basin till the close of the war."[1] The cart had large, solid wooden wheels, made by slicing a circular disk from the butt of a huge log. The hub was usually about three feet from the ground, permitting the cart to go anywhere the oxen could pull it.

Wagon freighting had begun in earnest across the Alleghenies by about 1785. As a consequence, road building began, in a sense, at that time. It started at the centers of population and spread slowly westward along the arteries of trade. Merchandise was carried by wagons as far as the passable roads extended, then it was transferred to pack-animals and forwarded still farther over the bridle paths.[2]

The rough country was not conducive to improved vehicles. The different types of wagons and coaches were usually simple and in many cases crude. It is the purpose of this chapter to mention a few of the more important of these vehicles and give brief descriptions of them. According to William Darby, there were a few improvements by

[1] "Evolution of a Road from Indian Trail to Modern Highway," *Road Economics*, Vol. V (1924), No. 10, pp. 11, 12.
[2] *Ibid.*

the year 1818. He described conditions by stating, "Except by water, there are no public conveniences yet established in the Mississippi or Mobile countries, for the convenience of travellers; they are obliged to provide themselves the means of transportation. Horses, of all prices, are constantly to be procured in New Orleans and Natchez, a medium price may be about eighty dollars."[3]

One authority, discussing early transportation conditions stated that

From village to village, pathways are formed, wheel-carriages are invented to gather the fruits of harvest, and they wear their own paths upon the surface of the soil, and finally the road is constructed, more or less perfect, as a means of transport between places more or less distant. In such a state of affairs the roads are very imperfect, and the carriages of the rudest description. It is conceivable that the first step from the pack-horse and its pathway, to the two-wheeled cart and a road was a very great advance—nearly as much as from the road to the railway.[4]

In America, during this period, two general classes of vehicles were in common service; first, the one used in the settled areas, and second, those used on the frontier. The former, being a more fragile type, never ventured beyond the limits of the settlement and therefore did not play a part in the great migration. The latter was heavily constructed and as varied as the conditions that gave rise to them.

The heavy wagon was employed when the entire household was being moved. It was the type known as the Conestoga wagon which later became known as the "covered wagon" on the western plains. This style of wagon was first made in the Conestoga Valley of Lancaster County, Pennsylvania and was of such excellent design that the name became famous throughout the country, and the wagons be-

[3] Darby, *The Emigrant's Guide*, p. 43.
[4] *Eighty Years' Progress of the United States*, II, 172.

A Southern Wagon showing Conestoga Influence. From *The Conestoga Six-Horse Bell Teams*, by John Omwake.

came known as Conestogas. "They were designed and built by local wheelwrights out of swamp oak, white oak, hickory, locust and poplar, from the neighboring woodlands, and were ironed by the village blacksmiths."[5]

A Conestoga wagon was huge and heavily built, differing from its English prototype in that the bed was higher at each end than in the middle. The wagon bed had the concave shape in order that its contents, if they should shift when going up or down hill, would not spill out but would settle toward the middle and not press against the end gate. The bows that held the white homespun cover followed the line of the ends of the body, slanted outward and gave a distinctive and unmistakable silhouette. "The top of the front hoop was eleven feet from the ground. The white homespun cover was two dozen feet long. The top ends of the wagon bed were sixteen feet apart and the rear wheels five or six feet high. When the six-horse team was pulling, the team and wagon stretched to sixty feet."[6] Another distinguishing characteristic of the conveyance was its color. "The under body was always painted blue, and the upper woodwork was invariably bright red. This chromatic scheme was as inevitable for every Conestoga wagon as though it had been prescribed by law with a penalty for refusal so to decorate."[7] Being sturdily built the Conestoga wagon could withstand a great amount of hardships and therefore won its place among those vehicles that were used in shipping merchandise.

Another type, similar to the heavy wagon, in that it was used to transfer goods, was the little Jersey wagon. This wagon was much lighter in construction than the Conestoga and was suitable primarily for local traveling. While both wagons were used in the transportation of freight, the Cones-

[5] John Omwake, *The Conestoga Six-Horse Bell Teams*, p. 17.
[6] *Ibid.* [7] Dunbar, *op. cit.*, I, 203, 204.

toga was employed when all the possessions of a household were being moved to a new home; the Jersey wagon, when travelers did not find it necessary to carry many belongings with them. The Jersey wagon was sometimes called a "dearborn" and other times a "carry all."[8]

The stage-coach, "so called because journeys in those days were accomplished by successive stages, after each of which the horses were invariably changed, and occasionally the coach as well,"[9] was a familiar sight on the roads in the South. It was built to carry nine persons inside, and the driver's seat would accommodate three more, including the driver. The body of the coach stood about three and a half feet from the ground. The rear wheels were five feet high and the front ones about three and a half feet. The body was swung on straps from iron braces that were fitted to the axles and had no springs. The inside was lined with leather and plush. That much jostling about ensued when the horses were moving along at a lively rate over rough ground was proved by the fact that the rear seat was fitted with a breast strap. Each side of the coach was fitted with a door containing a small pane of glass. The remainder of the body—except front and back, which were paneled—was enclosed with leather curtains which could be rolled up. When the doors were opened, steps were let down from the bottom of the body.[10] The driver sat up in front and on the rear was a rack for luggage.[11] Accidents were frequent, delays long, and the ride very uncomfortable. Breaking an axle was a common occurrence, but the lives of the passengers were safe, because the conditions of the roads prevented

---

[8] Hodgson, *op. cit.*, I, 119-20.

[9] G. W. W. Houghton, *The Hub's Vocabulary of Vehicles*, p. 20.

[10] Labert St. Clair, *Since Time began Transportation—Land, Air, Water*, pp. 59, 60.

[11] James Logan, *Notes of a Journey through Canada, the United States of America, and the West Indies*, p. 171.

the coach from going at a rapid rate. In crossing streams it was often necessary for the occupants of the stage to draw their feet up underneath them in order that they might not be dragged through the water. Then again the coach would reel, pitch, and toss so that at times it would be unbearable, and walking was preferred—though a handsome price had been paid for the trip.

The mail stage-coach was of the same type except that it was built to serve a different purpose, the transportation of mail, and only secondarily, the conveyance of passengers.[12] They were usually light carriages fitted for the accommodation of nine persons, whose luggage and trunks were secured at the rear by means of a leather strap, in the same manner as it was done on the regular stage-coach. In the summer this carriage was agreeable, but in winter it was uncomfortable as there was "no other protection against the weather than a curtain of leather, often fastened in a negligent manner to the posts which support the roof."[13] The body of the coach was large and full paneled "with boots before and behind,"[14] and many had accommodations on the roof for passengers and luggage. The gear consisted of "low, stout wheels, heavy axles known as 'mail axles,' and it was at first suspended on thoroughbraces, and afterwards on telegraph springs."[15]

The mail coaches of 1799 were decorated, by order of Joseph Habersham, as follows:

The body painted green, colors formed of Prussian blue and yellow ochre; carriage and wheels red, lead mixed to approach vermilion as near as may be; octagon panel in the back, black; octagon blends green; elbow piece on rail, front rail and back, red as above; on all doors, Roman capitals in patent yellow,

---

[12] Thomas Hamilton, *op. cit.*, pp. 368, 380.
[13] D. B. Warden, *Statistical, Political, and Historical Account of the United States of North America*, I, 344.
[14] Houghton, *op. cit.*, p. 20.   [15] *Ibid.*

'United States Mail Stage' and over these words a spread eagle of size and color to suit.[16]

"The coaches were usually run either by a company or by individuals who derived most of their profit from a Government contract for carrying the mails, and they troubled themselves little about the passengers' comfort."[17] The post coaches were of two general types, the four-horse coach and the two-horse coach.[18] The requirements in connection with transportation of mail have been discussed in the chapter dealing with post-roads.

The earlier types of vehicles were all modifications of European types. It was necessary to make them suitable for the new and ungraded roads of America. Besides these European ones there were two Americanized types, the first of which was called a chair, and the other, a chaise. "The chair was a two-wheeled vehicle with a seat for two, and sometimes with an additional small seat, almost over the shafts, for the driver."[19] Locally this conveyance was called a "cheer." They were the only ones seen in the rural districts; the cost of such conveyances was no inconsiderable sum. "They were all hung upon springs made of wood generally, with rude bow or standing-top of round iron, hung around with painted cloth curtains. The linings and cushions, stuffed with 'swingling tow,' sometimes salt hay, were in those primitive times of simplicity and innocence deemed good enough for any American sovereign, and very fortunate was he who could get even a short ride in one!"[20] The chaise was simply a chair with a covered top of leather.[21] None of the earliest specimens of the chairs or

[16] H. M. Konwiser, *Colonial and Revolutionary Posts*, p. 63.
[17] Lathrop, *op. cit.*, p. 230.
[18] *American State Papers, Post Office*, p. 349.
[19] Dunbar, *op. cit.*, I, 46.
[20] Ezra M. Stratton, *The World on Wheels, or Carriages*, pp. 418-19.
[21] Dunbar, *op. cit.; Colonial Records of Georgia*, XIII, 535.

chaises had springs, but swung, as did the bodies of the stages, on stout branches of wood or leather that somewhat alleviated the constant jolting.

In addition to these more or less standard types of conveyance there were some unique examples. The most interesting one was mentioned in the Augusta (Georgia) *Chronicle* in the following manner:

> Emigration to the West. Passed through this place from Greenville District, bound for Chatahouchee, a man and his wife, his son and his wife with a cart but no horse. The man had a belt over his shoulders and he drew in the shafts—the son worked by traces tied to the end of the shafts and assisted his father to draw the cart; the son's wife rode in the cart, and the old woman was walking, carrying a rifle and driving a cow.[22]

Another odd carriage was described by Robert Sutcliffe. He had commented on the heavy traffic of the Lancaster Turnpike; he then made the following comparison:

> The appearance of things in the Slave States is quite the reverse of this. We sometimes meet a ragged black boy or girl driving a team consisting of a lean cow and a mule, sometimes a lean bull or an ox, and I have seen a bull and a cow, each miserable in its appearance, composing a team. . . . The carriage or wagon appeared in as wretched a condition as the team and its driver.[23]

This seems to have been the consensus of opinion everywhere in the South; bad roads gave rise to inadequate transportation facilities. Finlay said that "in this Province Travelling is most extravagantly expensive,"[24] especially when the quality of the vehicles and the condition of the roads were considered.

When Surveyor Finlay reached the Southern colonies he

---

[22] *Augusta* (Georgia) *Chronicle*, September 24, 1819, quoted in *Documentary History of American Industrial Society*, II, 196.

[23] *Travels in Some Parts of America in the Years 1804, 1805, 1806*, quoted in Richardson Wright, *Hawkers and Walkers in Early America*, p. 266.

[24] *Op. cit.* p. 52.

found that the terrible roads were made easier to bear only by the traditional Southern hospitality. "To travel with comfort through this part of the world, a stranger, shou'd be furnished with letters of recommendation to the Gentlemen and Planters living on the road, but to a man who has business to mind this method of travelling wou'd be attended with inconvenience for the hospitable Americans kill you with kindness."[25]

Along the roads leading to the west moved the cavalcade of vehicles. The low rumble of the wheels was broken periodically by the sharp crack of a whip or by a piercing cry from one of the drivers. Onward, onward they pushed through a valley inundated by a swollen stream, over a dividing ridge, and down into another valley.

Thus the Old Southwest was being penetrated during the first decade of the nineteenth century.

By a careful examination of the maps made during the years 1825 to 1830, one can accurately determine the sections most accessible at that time. Many roads and numerous towns were delineated by the cartographers in these areas. To contrast this with areas that were less accessible, examine the portions of the maps where little was depicted, few roads and sparse settlements being shown. What characterized this difference? Accessibility, nature of the land, and the desires of the immigrants, all had a part in determining the direction a road should take and where a town should be located.

It was the relative ease of travel along the fall line route, around the southern end of the Appalachian Mountains that stimulated movement into the lower South, enabling the southern territories to achieve statehood in rapid succession.

[25] *Ibid.*, quoted in *American Mails in 1773*, p. 3, published by the United States Post Office Department.

APPENDIX I

Exported from Georgia from 1790 to 1820

		Domestic	Foreign	Total
10-1-1790	to 9-30-1791			491,250
1791	1792			459,106
1792	1793			520,955
1793	1794			263,832
1794	1795			695,289
1795	1796			950,158
1796	1797			644,307
1797	1798			961,848
1798	1799			1,396,759
1799	1800			2,174,268
1800	1801			1,755,939
1801	1802			1,854,951
1802	1803	2,345,387	25,488	2,370,875
1803	1804	2,003,227	74,345	2,077,572
1804	1805	2,351,169	43,677	2,394,846
1805	1806	82,764	...	82,764
1806	1807	3,710,776	34,069	3,744,845
1807	1808	24,626	...	24,626
1808	1809	1,082,108	...	1,082,108
1809	1810	2,234,912	3,774	2,238,686
1810	1811	2,557,225	11,641	2,568,866
1811	1812	1,066,703	...	1,066,703
1812	1813	1,094,595	...	1,094,595
1813	1814	2,147,449	35,672	2,183,121
1814	1815	4,146,057	26,262	4,172,319
1815	1816	7,436,692	75,237	7,511,929
1816	1817	8,530,831	259,883	8,790,714
1817	1818	10,977,051	155,045	11,132,096
1818	1819	6,241,960	68,474	6,310,434
1819	1820	6,525,013	69,610	6,594,623

No returns received from District of Savannah for the year 1807-1808.[1]

[1] *American State Papers, Commerce and Navigation*, I, 489, 507, 544, 591, 672, 697, 722, 739, 816, 870, 893, 927, 966, 995, 1023; II, 23, 56, 96, 159, 329, 470.

EXPORTED FROM MISSISSIPPI FROM 1806-1820

Mississippi (Mobile)

		Domestic	Foreign	Total
10-1-1806 to	9-30-1807	701		701
1807	1808			
1808	1809	305		305
1809	1810	2,958		2,958
1810	1811	1,441		1,441
1811	1812	3,107		3,107

Mississippi Territory

1813	1814	76,929		76,929
1814	1815	2,573		2,573
1815	1816	8,232		8,232
1816	1817	43,887		43,887

Mississippi

1817	1818	84,764	12,093	96,857
1818	1819	50,456	450	50,906
1819	1820	96,636		96,636[2]

[2] *Ibid.*, I, 722, 816, 870, 893, 966, 1023; II, 23, 56, 96, 159, 389, 470.

Exported from New Orleans, Louisiana, from 1804 to 1820

		Domestic	Foreign	Total
1-30-1804 to	9-30-1804	1,392,093	208,269	1,600,362
10-1-1804	9-30-1805	2,338,483	1,033,062	3,371,545
1805	1806	2,357,141	1,530,182	3,887,323
1806	1807	3,161,381	1,159,174	4,320,555
1807	1808	537,711	723,390	1,261,101
1808	1809	344,303	197,621	541,924
1809	1810	1,753,974	136,978	1,890,952
1810	1811	2,501,842	148,208	2,650,050
1811	1812	1,025,602	34,869	1,060,471
1812	1813	1,013,667	31,486	1,045,153
1813	1814	383,709	3,482	387,191
1814	1815	5,055,858	46,752	5,102,610
1815	1816	5,251,833	351,115	5,602,948
1816	1817	8,241,254	783,558	9,024,812
1817	1818	12,176,910	747,399	12,924,309
1818	1819	8,950,921	817,832	9,768,753
1819	1820	7,242,415	353,742	7,596,157[8]

[8] *Ibid.*, I, 591, 672, 697, 722, 739, 816, 870, 893, 966, 995, 1023; II, 23, 56, 96, 159, 389, 470.

APPENDIX II

INNS AND TAVERNS

An Annotated List,
Geographically and Chronologically Arranged.

Georgia

Savannah—
1. "House for Strangers."[1] (1734) South side of St. Julian, second door east of Whitaker Street.
2. Tavern, Townsend's.[2] (1738)
3. Public-House, Jenkins'.[3] (1738-41)
4. Public House, Penrose's.[4] (1740-41)
5. Tavern, Fallowfield's.[5] (1740).
6. Tavern, Mrs. Eppinger's.[6] (1747-85) Northeast corner Jefferson and South Broad.
7. Tavern, Mrs. Mary Smith.[7] (1763-64)
8. Tavern, Matthias Ash.[8] (1764)
9. Tavern, George Dresler.[9] (1764)
10. Tavern, John Perkins.[10] (1764)
11. Tavern, Abigail Minis.[11] (1764)
12. Tavern, George Ducker.[12] (1764)
13. Tavern, Andrew Stuart.[13] (1764)
14. Tavern, James Machenery.[14] (1764)

[1] F. D. Lee and J. L. Agnew, *Historical Record of the City of Savannah*, p. 10. Shown on map of town drawn by Peter Gordon.
[2] *Colonial Records of Georgia*, IV, 61-62, 111.
[3] *Ibid.*, XXII (pt. 2), 17, 84, 142, 406, 427, 428.
[4] *Ibid.*, Supplement to IV, 34, 130.
[5] *Ibid.*, p. 50.
[6] *Gazette of the State of Georgia*, No. 152; Adelaide Wilson, *Historic and Picturesque Savannah*, p. 90; Lee and Agnew, *op. cit.*, p. 72, footnote.
[7] *Georgia Gazette*, Nos. 2, 3, 45, 49, 95, 97.
[8] *Georgia Gazette*, Nos. 44, 46, 95, 97, 172, 176.
[9] *Ibid.*
[10] *Ibid.*, Nos. 44, 46.
[11] *Ibid.*, Nos. 44, 46, 95, 97, 172, 176.
[12] *Ibid.*, Nos. 45, 46, 95, 97.
[13] *Ibid.*, Nos. 44, 46.
[14] *Ibid.*, Nos. 44, 46, 64, 95, 97, 136, 176.

APPENDIX

15. Tavern, Adam Eirik.[15] (1764)
16. Tavern, Benjamin Wilson.[16] (1764)
17. Tavern, Alexander Creighton.[17] (1764-67)
18. Tavern, John Bowles.[18] (1764)
19. Tavern, John Lyon.[19] (1765)
20. Tavern, Daniel Ocain.[20] (1766)
21. Tavern, Mary O'Neal.[21] (1767)
22. Tavern, Garret Allen.[22] (1767)
23. Tavern, Tondee's.[23] (1774) Northwest corner Whitaker and Broughton Streets.
24. Boarding-House, Dillon's.[24] (1779)
25. Oyster House.[25] (1784)
26. Tavern, Aaron Moore.[26] (1784)
27. Savannah Tavern.[27] (1784)
28. Tavern, Murray's.[28] (1784)
29. Tavern, Alexander Allison.[29] (1784-85)
30. Boarding-house, Mrs. Macfarlane's.[30] (1785) Broughton Street.
31. Tavern, Widow M'Knight's.[31] (1785)
32. Savannah Coffee House, Burt and Stebbins.[32] (1785-91) Opened November 17, 1785 and was situated "on the bay."
33. Boarding house, Jane Griggs.[33] (1785) Located at Yamacraw.

[15] *Ibid.*, Nos. 95, 97; (Spelled "Irick" in Nos. 172, 176.)
[16] *Ibid.*, Nos. 95, 97.
[17] *Ibid.*, Nos. 95, 97, 110, 150, 176, 211.
[18] *Ibid.*, Nos. 95, 97.
[19] *Ibid.*, Nos. 103, 132, 163, 170.   [21] *Ibid.*, Nos. 172, 176.
[20] *Ibid.*, No. 144.   [22] *Ibid.*
[23] Charles Colcock Jones, *History of Georgia*, II, 151-53; Elise Lathrop, *Early American Inns and Taverns*, p. 229; Wilson, *op. cit.*, p. 43; Lee and Agnew, *op. cit.*, pp. 34, 35, 37.
[24] *Travels of John Davis in the United States of America, 1798-1802*, I, 123.
[25] *Gazette of the State of Georgia*, No. 50.
[26] *Ibid.*, No. 51.
[27] *Ibid.*, March 4, 1784, quoted in Wilson, *op. cit.*, p. 72.
[28] *Gazette of the State of Georgia*, Nos. 65, 66.
[29] *Ibid.*, Nos. 90-94, 101, 111-17, 125-28, 142.
[30] *Ibid.*, Nos. 108-10.
[31] *Ibid.*, Nos. 111, 112.
[32] *Ibid.*, Nos. 144, 147, 167-69; John Pope, *A Tour through the Southern and Western Territories of the United States of North America*, p. 79.
[33] *Gazette of the State of Georgia*, Nos. 118-20.

34. State Hotel, Wm. Thompson.[34] (1786) Opened January 16, 1786 and was situated "on the bay."
35. Tavern, Ring's.[35] (1786)
36. Brown's Coffee House.[36] (1791)
37. Tavern.[37] (1791) Located at the corner of Barnard and State Streets, replaced by Odd Fellows' Hall.
38. Inn, Eppinger.[38] South Broad Street, three doors east of Drayton.
39. City Tavern.[39] (1798) Christopher Gunn. On Broughton Street.
40. Screven House.[40] Began as Mrs. Platt's boarding house, Johnson Square. In 1869 R. Bradley & Sons were the proprietors.
41. Washington Hall.[41] (1812) Corner Jefferson and Bay Streets.
42. Georgia Hotel.[42] (1812)
43. Exchange Coffee House.[43] (1825)
44. Tavern, Mrs. Maxwell's.[44] (1825) Where Lafayette stayed while in Savannah.
45. Mrs. Battey's boarding house.[45] (1838) Across the square from Mrs. Platt's.
46. City Hotel.[46] Captain Wiltberger. (1838-55) Bay Street between Bull and Whitaker Streets.

[34] *Ibid.*, Nos. 155-159, 167, 168, 178, 181-186; Wilson, *op. cit.*, p. 71.
[35] *Gazette of the State of Georgia*, Nos. 204, 205.
[36] *Washington's Diary*, IV, 176; Archibald Henderson, *Washington's Southern Tour*, pp. 208, 209, 217; Wilson, *op. cit.*, p. 92; Lee and Agnew, *op. cit.*, p. 70.
[37] *Washington's Diary*, IV, 176; Henderson, *op. cit.*, p. 208; Wilson, *op. cit.*, p. 91; Lee and Agnew, *op. cit.*, p. 70, designated as St. James Square.
[38] Wilson, *op. cit.*, p. 90. This Eppinger was the grandson of the original Eppinger. The Tavern (No. 32) was occupied as a residence when this inn was opened.
[39] *Ibid.*, pp. 101, 125.
[40] *Ibid.*, pp. 152, 153; Lee and Agnew, *op. cit.*, p. 160.
[41] Wilson, *op. cit.*, p. 125.
[42] *Ibid.*, pp. 113, 125.
[43] *Ibid.*, p. 119; Lee and Agnew, *op. cit.*, p. 77.
[44] *An Account of the Reception of General Lafayette*, p. 20.
[45] Wilson, *op. cit.*, pp. 152, 153.
[46] *Ibid.*, p. 154; Thomas Gamble, *Savannah Duels and Duelists, 1733-1877*, p. 211.

APPENDIX 145

47. Pulaski House.⁴⁷ Captain Wiltberger. (1838-54) Northwest corner of Bull and Bryan Streets including Mrs. Battey's boarding house.
48. Mansion House.⁴⁸ Captain Wiltberger. (1838) Northwest corner Broughton and Whitaker Streets.
49. Irving House.⁴⁹ Alexander Irving, Proprietor. (1869) Corner Jefferson and St. Julian Streets.
50. Marshall House.⁵⁰ (1869)

Augusta—
1. Tavern, James Jarvis.⁵¹ (1763)
2. Coffee House.⁵² (1798)
3. Boarding House, Mrs. Longstreet.⁵³ (1805)
4. Globe Tavern.⁵⁴ (1816-78) Broad and Jackson Streets.
5. Mansion House.⁵⁵ (1819-27) Opened October 1, 1819 under the management of Young and MacKeene and in 1821 it was operated by Robert M'Keen. Corner Green and M'Intosh Streets.
6. Planters' Hotel.⁵⁶ (1819-53) In 1819 located on North side, upper end, Broad Street and operated by Crosby Dickinson and Ebenezer Starnes. In 1821 operated by John Miller and located on Jones Street between Reynolds and Macarten Streets.
7. City Hotel.⁵⁷ (1821) Edward Byrd and James R. Danforth.

⁴⁷ Wilson, *op. cit.*, p. 152; Gamble, *op. cit.*, pp. 192, 194, 210, Illustration, p. 193; Lee and Agnew, *op. cit.*, pp. 78, 129, 160.
⁴⁸ Wilson, *op. cit.*, p. 152.
⁴⁹ Lee and Agnew, *op. cit.*, p. 4 of the advertisements.
⁵⁰ *Ibid.*, p. 160.
⁵¹ *Georgia Gazette*, No. 44.
⁵² *Minutes of the Trustees of the University of Georgia, 1786-1817*, pp. 1-11, quoted in E. M. Coulter, *College Life in the Old South*, p. 8.
⁵³ John Wade, *Augustus Baldwin Longstreet*, p. 20.
⁵⁴ Henry Ker, *Travels through the Western Interior of the United States*, p. 345; J. T. Derry, *Georgia*, p. vii; Adiel Sherwood, *Gazetteer of the State of Georgia* (1827), pp. 27, 28; Sherwood, *op. cit.* (1837), p. 123.
⁵⁵ *Georgia Advertiser* (Augusta), III (1821), p. 259; Sherwood, *op. cit.* (1827); *Augusta Chronicle and Georgia Gazette*, XXXIII (1819), No. 1748.
⁵⁶ *Georgia Advertiser*, *op. cit.*; *Augusta Chronicle and Georgia Gazette*, XXXIII (1819), No. 1697; Jane M. C. and Marion Turnbull, *American Photographs*, II, 81; Derry, *op. cit.*, illustration p. 60, advertisement p. vii; Sherwood, *op. cit.* (1827); Sherwood, *op. cit.* (1837), p. 123.
⁵⁷ *Georgia Advertiser* (Augusta), III (1821), 259; Sherwood, *op. cit.*

8. Tavern.[58] (1825) Formerly occupied by Captain James Abercrombie, now run by B. Long.
9. Eagle Tavern.[59] (1827)
10. United States Tavern.[60] (1837)
11. Phoenix Hotel.[61] (1837)

Milledgeville—
1. House of Public Entertainment.[62] (1810) Thomas G. Collier. Facing the Public Square.
2. House of Entertainment.[63] (1810) Samuel Buffington.
3. Eagle Tavern.[64] (1811-1829) Peter Thomas and Peter Gent. Before November 6, 1811 this tavern was run by Roger Olmstead. Wayne Street, midway between Greene and Hancock.
4. Tavern.[65] (1811) Jabez Roberts. The tavern had been previously run by David Flucker and at another time by Henry Darned. Facing the State House.
5. House of Entertainment.[66] (1811). John Downer. East corner of State House Square.
6. Public House.[67] (1811) Thomas Parting.
7. Tavern.[68] (1820)

Athens—
1. Easley's House, Daniel Easley.[69] (1801) The only dwelling "in town."
2. Meigs' House, Josiah Meigs.[70] (1801) He turned his home into a tavern.
3. Planters' Hotel.[71] (1830)
4. Globe Tavern.[72]

[58] *Alabama Journal*, I, November 25, 1825.
[59] Sherwood, *op. cit.* (1827); Sherwood, *op. cit.* (1837), p. 123.
[60] *Ibid.*
[61] *Ibid.*
[62] *Georgia Journal* (Milledgeville), I (1810), Nos. 41, 49.
[63] *Ibid.*, No. 49.
[64] *Ibid.*, III (1811), No. 2; Sherwood, *op. cit.*, p. 134.
[65] *Georgia Journal* (Milledgeville), I (1810), No. 2.
[66] *Ibid.*
[67] *Georgia Journal* (Milledgeville), III (1811), No. 2.
[68] Adam Hodgson, *Letters from North America*, I, 111.
[69] Coulter, *op. cit.*, pp. 10, 16.
[70] *Ibid.*, p. 16.   [71] *Ibid.*, p. 299.   [72] *Ibid.*

APPENDIX 147

5. Franklin Hotel.[73] (1830-59) Formerly the Athens Hotel. In 1831 its name was changed to Georgia Hotel. In 1838 when the railroads was nearing Athens from Augusta, this *hotel being the closest to the proposed terminus,* changed its name again to Rail Road House. Still later the name was changed to Lanier House.
6. French Boarding House, G. L. Jules D'Antel.[74] (1845)
7. Newton House.[75] (1854)

Southwest Road out of Savannah, Christ Church Parish—
1. Tavern, John Barnes.[76] (1763)
2. Tavern, James Tebaut.[77] (1763-64)
3. Tavern, Thomas White.[78] (1764)

Sunbury, St. John's Parish—
1. Tavern, High Clark.[79] (1764-67)
2. Tavern, Abraham Williams.[80] (1764)
3. Tavern, Nathaniel Yates.[81] (1767)
4. Tavern, Richard Buntly.[82] (1767)
5. Tavern, James Rutherford.[83] (1767)

Northwest Road out of Savannah—
1. Tavern, Cotlieb Stehle.[84] (1763-67) In St. Matthew Parish 10 miles from Savannah.
2. Tavern, Catherine Zetler.[85] (1763-64) In St. Matthew Parish.
3. Tavern, Robert Bevil.[86] (1764) In St. Matthew Parish.
4. Tavern, Martin Dasher.[87] (1764) Ebenezer, St. Matthew Parish.
5. Tavern, John Rentz.[88] (1764) Ebenezer, St. Matthew Parish.
6. Tavern, John Flerl.[89] (1767) At the mill four miles below Ebenezer, St. Matthew Parish.
7. Tavern, Francis Goffe.[90] (1767) In Christ Church Parish one mile from Savannah.

[73] *Ibid.,* pp. 185, 299.
[74] *Ibid.,* p. 270.
[75] *Ibid.,* p. 185.
[76] *Georgia Gazette,* No. 44.
[77] *Ibid.,* Nos. 44, 95.
[78] *Ibid.,* No. 95.
[79] *Ibid.,* Nos. 95, 172, 176.
[80] *Ibid.,* No. 95.
[81] *Ibid.,* Nos. 172, 176.
[82] *Ibid.,* No. 176.
[83] *Ibid.*
[84] *Ibid.,* Nos. 44, 95, 176.
[85] *Ibid.,* Nos. 44, 95.
[86] *Ibid.,* No. 95.
[87] *Ibid.*
[88] *Ibid.*
[89] *Ibid.,* No. 176.
[90] *Ibid.,* Nos. 172, 176.

8. Sign of the King's Arms, John Bowles.[91] (1768) One half mile from Savannah.
9. Tavern, Pace's.[92] (1775) Located at the Two Sisters' Bluff.
10. Tavern, Herbert's.[93] (1775) St. George's Parish.
11. Dacres Tavern.[94] (1780) Goshen Church near Abercorn.
12. Tavern, Powell's.[95] (1785-1810) In Effingham county 18 miles from Savannah.
13. Tavern, Spencer's.[96] (1791) Fifteen miles from Savannah.
14. Tavern, Russel's.[97] (1791) Fifteen miles from Spencer's.
15. Tavern, Garnet's.[98] (1791) Nineteen miles from Russel's.
16. Tavern, Pierce's.[99] (1791-1806) Eight miles from Garnet's.
17. Tavern, Spinner's.[100] (1791) Seventeen miles from Pierce's.
18. Tavern, Lambert's.[101] (1791) Thirteen miles from Spinner's.
19. Tavern.[102] (1791) Waynesbrough, fourteen miles from Lambert's. This town was the county seat of Burkes county.
20. Hely's Inn.[103] (1806) Fifteen miles from Savannah.
21. Tavern, Berry's.[104] (1806) Thirteen miles from Hely's Inn.
22. Tavern, Major King's.[105] (1806) Ten miles from Berry's.
23. Tavern, Scrogg's.[106] (1806) Ten miles from Major King's.
24. Tavern, Burrel's.[107] (1806) Thirty miles from Scrogg's.
25. Tavern, Widow Laseter's.[108] (1806) Eighteen miles from Burrel's.
26. Tavern, Wynne's.[109] (1806) Located in Waynesbrough four miles from Widow Laseter's.
27. Tavern.[110] (1806) Louisville.
28. Inn, Posner's.[111] (1806) Richmond Springs twenty-eight miles from Louisville.

[91] *Ibid.*, No. 266.
[92] *Documentary History of American Industrial Society*, II, 279.
[93] *Ibid.*, p. 280.
[94] Campbell (Map), *Sketch of the Northern Frontier of Georgia.*
[95] *Gazette of the State of Georgia*, No. 151; John Melish, *Travels through the United States of America*, p. 262.
[96] *Washington's Diary*, IV, 178.
[97] *Ibid.*
[98] *Ibid.*
[99] *Ibid.*; Melish, *op. cit.*, p. 41.
[100] *Washington's Diary*, IV, 178.
[101] *Ibid.*
[102] *Ibid.*
[103] Melish, *op. cit.*, p. 39.
[104] *Ibid.*, pp. 40, 52.
[105] *Ibid.*
[106] *Ibid.*, p. 40.
[107] *Ibid.*, p. 41.
[108] *Ibid.*, p. 43.
[109] *Ibid.*, p. 44.
[110] *Ibid.*, pp. 46, 47.
[111] *Ibid.*, p. 49.

APPENDIX   149

29. Twenty-three Mile House.[112] (1819) Wilson Navey, on the road from Augusta to Savannah.
30. Tavern, Jones'.[113] (1810) Sixty-two miles from Savannah.
31. Three Taverns, Madison.[114] (1810)
32. Tavern, Madison Springs.[115] (1826)
33. Tavern.[116] (1828) Mrs. Fulton. Twenty-four miles south of Savannah.
34. Tavern.[117] (1828) Ricebrough.
35. Tavern.[118] (1828) Mr. Golden's. Twenty miles west of Ricebrough.
36. Tavern.[119] (1828) Mr. Rick's.
37. Tavern.[120] (1828) Mrs. O'Niel's. Twenty-nine miles west of Mr. Rick's Tavern.
38. Tavern.[121] Mrs. Wells'. (1828) Between the Flint and the Chatahoochee Rivers.

Road from Augusta to Columbus—
1. Tavern, Mrs. Harris'.[122] (1820) Twenty-eight miles from Augusta.
2. Tavern.[123] (1820) Twelve miles from Mrs. Harris'.
3. Tavern, Shiver's.[124] (1820) Located on the Ogechee River forty-five miles from Mrs. Harris'.
4. "House of Entertainment for Travellers," Fort Hawkins.[125] (1820)
5. Inn.[126] (1820) Indian Agency on the Flint River.
6. Inn, Spaine's.[127] (1820) Twenty-eight miles from the Agency.
7. Tavern.[128] (1828) "Hotel signs swing among the trees and we were very well accomodated at the principal one."

[112] *Augusta Chronicle and Georgia Gazette*, XXXIII (1819), No. 1694.
[113] Melish, *op. cit.*, p. 262.
[114] *Ibid.*, p. 264.
[115] *Life and Letters of Stephen Olin*, I, 133; Coulter, *op. cit.*, p. 68.
[116] Mrs. Basil Hall, *The Aristocratic Journey*, p. 229.
[117] *Ibid.*, pp. 234, 235.
[118] *Ibid.*, p. 235.
[119] *Ibid.*, p. 236.
[120] *Ibid.*
[121] *Ibid.*, pp. 236, 238.
[122] Hodgson, *op. cit.*, I, 107.
[123] *Ibid.*, p. 108.
[124] *Ibid.*, p. 109.
[125] *Ibid.*, p. 114.
[126] *Ibid.*, p. 115.
[127] *Ibid.*, p. 117.
[128] Hall, *op. cit.*, p. 240.

8. House of Entertainment.[129] (1819) William M'Intosh and Peter Donaldson. Mineral Springs, Creek Nation, fifteen miles from Monticello, Jasper County, Georgia.
9. Tavern.[130] (1819) William and David Boren. Washington, Wilkes County, Georgia. Lately occupied by Mr. Holliday, previously by Daniel Stone.
10. Indian Queen Tavern.[131] (1828) Columbus, operated by George W. Dillard.
11. Tavern.[132] (1835-36) Columbus.
12. Tavern.[133] (1835) Sparta.
13. Mansion House.[134] (1826) Macon. Recently occupied by Bullock and Wells and formerly by Wm. Bivins and now occupied again by Wm. Bivins.
14. Hotel.[135] (1836) Macon.

ALABAMA

Montgomery—
1. Tavern.[136] First one in Montgomery. North side of Decatur, then Market Street.
2. Globe Tavern.[137] (18 -1830) North side of Main Street opposite the market. This establishment was built two years after the first Tavern was built. Before 1825 it was occupied by Benjamin Williamson and at this date it was called the Indian Queen and was operated by Micajah Williamson. In 1827 the name was changed to the Globe Tavern or "At the Sign of the Globe" and was operated by Lewis Calffrey. In 1830 it was burned down.
3. Mansion House.[138] (1821-59) Later succeeded by the Exchange Hotel.

---

[129] *Augusta Chronicle and Georgia Gazette*, XXXIII (1819), No. 1752.
[130] *Ibid.*, No. 1713.
[131] *Alabama Journal*, III, May 23, 1828.
[132] G. W. Featherstonhough, *Excursion through the Slave States*, II, 320, 321; James Logan, *Notes of a Journey through Canada, the United States of America, and the West Indies*, p. 172; Hall, *op. cit.*, p. 240.
[133] Featherstonhough, *op. cit.*, II, 329; Thomas Hamilton, *Men and Manners in America*, p. 381.
[134] *Alabama Journal*, II, Dec. 8, 1826.
[135] Logan, *op. cit.*, p. 172.
[136] Lathrop, *op. cit.*, p. 231.
[137] *Ibid.; Alabama Journal*, I, Nov. 25, 1825; II, June 29, July 27, 1827.
[138] Lathrop, *op. cit.;* Turnbull, *op. cit.*, II, 69; Charles Mackay, *Life and Liberty in America*, p. 186.

APPENDIX 151

4. Montgomery Hotel.[139] (1825-30) In 1826 the hotel was known as the Bell Tavern and was operated by B. W. Bell. Later it was operated by J. S. Bailey, and in 1828 it was sold to J. B. Clopton who was assisted by T. W. Livingston. Later this tavern was called the Lafayette Tavern.
5. House of Private Entertainment.[140] (1825) Court Street. Formerly occupied by Andrew M'Bryde and now operated by Marble Stone.
6. Farmers' and Planters' Hotel.[141] (1826) Operated by Mungin and Saunders.
7. Montgomery Arms.[142]
8. Montgomery Inn.[143] (1828) Formerly occupied by E. D. Washburn and now by J. D. Whetstone. Situated opposite store of Messrs. Wm. and P. D. Sayre.
9. Union Hotel.[144] (1831-32) Situated on Commerce Street between the Public Square and Steamboat landing, opposite Post Office. The proprietors in 1831 were Jordain Peters and J. W. Freeman, and in 1832 it was purchased by Z. T. Watkins.
10. Planters' Hotel.[145] (1831) Previously occupied by James Pritchard and now operated by Hubbell and Shelton.
11. Eagle and Phoenix Hotel.[146] (1832) Situated on the site of the old City Hotel on Broad Street. Operated by Cosnard and Byrd.

Road between Mobile and Fort Mitchell.
1. Tavern.[147] (1820-24) Located at Ouchee Bridge.
2. Tavern.[148] (1820-36) Fort Bainbridge. From 1820-24 it was kept by Capt. Kendall Lewis, by 1830 it was kept by a Mrs. Harris, and in 1836 it was known as Cook's Tavern.

[139] Lathrop, *op. cit.*, p. 231; Featherstonhough, *op. cit.*, II, 283; *Alabama Journal*, I, Feb. 17, 1826; II, Feb. 16, 1827, Nov. 28, 1828.
[140] *Alabama Journal*, I, Oct. 14, 1825.
[141] *Ibid.*, I, Feb. 3, 1826. [142] Logan, *op. cit.*, p. 175.
[143] *Alabama Journal*, II, March 14, April 11, 1828.
[144] *Ibid.*, VI, Sept. 24, 1831, Feb. 10, 1832.
[145] *Ibid.*, VI, Sept. 3, 1831. [146] *Ibid.*, VII, Sept. 29, 1832.
[147] Hodgson, *op. cit.*, I, 123; A. Levasseur, *Lafayette in America in 1824 and 1825*, II, 78; Lathrop, *op. cit.*, p. 230; G. W. Featherstonhough, *op. cit.*, II, 318.
[148] Lathrop, *op. cit.*, pp. 230, 231; Hodgson, *op. cit.*, I, 127; Levasseur, *op. cit.*, II, 80; Hamilton, *op. cit.*, p. 370; Hall, *op. cit.*, pp. 240, 241.

3. Bonum House.[149] (1820) Ten miles south of Montgomery.
4. Tavern.[150] (1820) Operated by Judge Burns, five miles from Blakely.
5. Tavern, Cooker's.[151] (1820)
6. Tavern.[152] (1820) Fort Dale.
7. Tavern.[153] (1820) "Kept by a Georgian." Beyond where the Mobile and Blakely roads fork.
8. Inn.[154] (1820) About forty miles beyond the fork of the Mobile and Blakely roads.
9. "House for paying guests."[155] (1820) Located at Leighton.
10. Tavern, Longmyre's.[156] (1820)
11. Tavern, Macdavid's.[157] (1820)
12. Tavern, Duncan MacMillan's.[158] (1820)
13. Tavern, Mrs. Mills'.[159] (1820)
14. Tavern, Peeble's.[160] (1820)
15. Tavern, Price's.[161] (1820)
16. Tavern.[162] (1820) Major Taylor.
17. Tavern.[163] (1820) Colonel Wood.
18. Tavern.[164] (1820) A log cabin near Colonel Wood's Tavern.
19. Gum Springs Tavern.[165] (1823) Near St. Stephens. Operated by David G. Jackson, recently operated by John Jacob Repsher.
20. Tavern.[166] (1824-40) On the banks of Line Creek.
21. House of Entertainment or Traveller's Rest.[167] (1825-26) Mount Pleasant, on road from Montgomery to Line Creek, 13 miles from Montgomery and 5 miles from Line Creek. Formerly occupied by Mr. Joseph H. Meigs, now operated by Colonel Clement Freeny.
22. Inn.[168] (1826) Monticello, Pike county. Operated by John Law.

[149] Lathrop, *op. cit.*, pp. 231, 232.
[150] *Ibid.*, p. 233.
[151] *Ibid.*, p. 232.
[152] *Ibid.*; Hodgson, *op. cit.*, I, 141, 142.
[153] Lathrop, *op. cit.*, p. 232.
[154] *Ibid.*
[155] *Ibid.*, p. 229.
[156] *Ibid.*, p. 232.
[157] *Ibid.*, p. 233.
[158] *Ibid.*, pp. 232, 233.
[159] *Ibid.*, p. 233.
[160] *Ibid.*
[161] *Ibid.*, p. 232.
[162] *Ibid.*
[163] *Ibid.*
[164] *Ibid.*
[165] *Mobile Argus*, I (1823), No. 75.
[166] Lathrop, *op. cit.*, p. 229; Levasseur, *op. cit.*, II, 81.
[167] *Alabama Journal*, I, Oct. 14, 1825, Jan. 6, 1826.
[168] *Ibid.*, Sept. 8, 1826.

APPENDIX 153

23. Tavern.[169] (1828) Capt. Triplett. 27 miles east of Montgomery.
24. Eagle Hotel.[170] (1828) Greensborough, Green county. Operated by Mrs. Elizabeth Alston.
25. LaFayette Hotel.[171] (1828) Greensborough, Green county. Operated by John Hillhouse.
26. Inn, Royston's.[172] (1830)
27. Tavern, Crowell's.[173] (1830-31)
28. Tavern.[174] (1830) Capt. Walker, Pole Cat Springs.
29. Eagle Hotel.[175] (1830) Greenville, Butler county. Operated by Samuel L. Caldwell.
30. Tavern.[176] (1831) Passamagoula.
31. Tavern.[177] (1831) On the road between Passamagoula and Mobile.
32. Inn.[178] (1832) Creek Stand in the Creek Nation, on the road from Columbus, Ga., to Montgomery, 38 miles from Montgomery. Operated by Sampson Lanier.
33. House of Entertainment, Walton's.[179] (1835)
34. Tavern, Macgirt's.[180] (1835)
35. Tavern.[181] (1836) Located in Tuskagee.

Mobile—
I. 1. Globe Hotel.[182] (1822-23) William P. Clark, after June 1, 1823 operated by Seth Stoddard.
2. U. S. Hotel.[183] (1822-25) Operated by John F. Everitt and later by W. Roberts. This may be the same hotel mentioned by Mrs. Hall, No. 5.

[169] Hall, *op. cit.*, p. 241.
[170] *Alabama Journal*, III, June 6, 1828.
[171] *Ibid.*, Aug. 22, 1828.
[172] Lathrop, *op. cit.*, p. 230.
[173] *Ibid.;* Hamilton, *op. cit.*, p. 375.
[174] Lathrop, *op. cit.*, p. 231.
[175] *Alabama Journal*, IV, March 12, 1830.
[176] Hamilton, *op. cit.*, pp. 359, 360.
[177] *Ibid.*, p. 360.
[178] *Alabama Journal*, VII, August 4, 1832.
[179] Featherstonhough, *op. cit.*, p. 314.
[180] *Ibid.*, p. 316; Hamilton, *op. cit.*, p. 374.
[181] Logan, *op. cit.*, pp. 174, 175.
[182] *Mobile Argus*, I (1822), No. 3, p. 55; *Cahawba Press and Alabama State Intelligencer*, III (1822), 33.
[183] *Mobile Argus*, I (1822), No. 6; *Alabama Journal*, I, Oct. 21, 1825.

3. Green House.[184] (1823) Opposite Mr. Pope's Hotel, Royal Street. Operated by James M. Prescott.
4. Alabama Hotel.[185] (1828-29) David White. A fire in 1827 burned most of the hotels in Mobile.
5. Tavern.[186] (1828) Mr. Robertson.
6. City Hotel.[187] (1829) John F. Everitt.
7. Public Boarding House.[188] (1829) Operated by Mrs. Brown.
8. Hotel.[189] (1835)
9. Battle House.[190] (1853-55)

Cahawba—
1. Cahawba House.[191] (1821) William Curtis. Vine and Arch Streets.
2. Boarding House.[192] (1821) Thomas Ewing. Located at First north street.
3. Boarding House.[193] (1821) M. Campbell and C. Humphreys.
4. Planters' Hotel.[194] (1821) James L. Baird. Second north and Mulberry Streets.
5. Hotel, Cox's.[195] (1821)
6. Inn.[196] (1831) Kahaba. Formerly kept by Samuel B. Ewing, lately by Mr. B. Robson, and now by Wm. Taylor.

Huntsville—
1. Hotel.[197] (1810) In Twickenham. John Read. Southwest corner of Square. A. Jameson and Allen Cooper.
2. Planters' Hotel.[198] (1820) N. B. Posey.

---

[184] *Mobile Argus*, I (1823), Oct. 31.
[185] Hall, *op. cit.*, p. 245; *Alabama Journal*, IV, Nov. 27, 1829.
[186] Hall, *op. cit.*, p. 246.
[187] *Alabama Journal*, IV, Sept. 18, 1829.
[188] *Ibid.*, Nov. 6, 1829.
[189] Featherstonhaugh, *op. cit.*, II, 277.
[190] Turnbull, *American Photographs*, II, 62; James Stirling, *Letters from the Slave States*, p. 179; Stirling, *The Sunny South*, p. 504.
[191] *Cahawba Press and Alabama State Intelligencer*, III (1821), 23.
[192] *Ibid.*   [194] *Ibid.*
[193] *Ibid.*   [195] *Ibid.*
[196] *Alabama Journal*, VI, Dec. 31, 1831.
[197] E. C. Betts, *Early History of Huntsville, Alabama*, p. 29.
[198] Huntsville *Alabama Republican*, Nov. 17, 1820, quoted in Betts, *op. cit.*, p. 76.

APPENDIX 155

3. Old Green Bottom Inn.[199] At Normal, Alabama, four miles south of Huntsville.

Tuscaloosa—
1. Eagle Hotel.[200] (1827) Formerly occupied by Major John B. Hogan, now operated by Samuel B. Ewing.
2. City Hotel.[201] (1828) Corner Broad and Market Streets. Operated by Whatley and McGuire.
3. Washington Hall.[202] (1832) Corner Broad and Market Streets. Operated by Samuel B. Ewing.

MISSISSIPPI
Natchez—
1. Hotel.[203] (1808)
2. Hotel.[204] (1820) Garnier.
3. Steamboat House.[205] (1833) Natchez Landing. Operated by Samuel Cotton.
4. Indian House.[206] (1833) Natchez (upper) landing. Operated by Isaac Jones.
5. Phepps' Hotel.[207] (1834) Lower end of Main Street.
6. Meridian Coffee House.[208] (1834) Main Street. Operated by Wells and Stevenson.
7. City Hotel.[209] (1835) Main Street. Operated by Halton and Barlow.
8. Bank Coffee House.[210] (1835) Main Street. Operated by F. Rowland.
9. Bell's Mansion House.[211] (1835-36) Wall and Franklin Streets.

[199] Betts, *op. cit.*, p. 33.
[200] *Alabama Journal*, II, June 8, 1827.
[201] *Ibid.*, II, Jan. 18, 1828.
[202] *Ibid.*, VII, Sept. 28, 1832.
[203] Christian Schultz, Jr., *Travels on an Inland Voyage through the States of New York, Pennsylvania, Virginia, Ohio, Kentucky, and Tennessee, . . . in the years 1807 and 1808*, II, 133.
[204] John James Audubon, *Delineations of American Scenery and Character*, p. 333.
[205] Smith and Wooster, *Mississippi and Louisiana Almanac . . . 1833*.
[206] *Ibid.*
[207] Vose, *Mississippi and Louisiana Almanac . . . 1835*.
[208] *Ibid.*
[209] *Ibid., 1836*.
[210] *Ibid.*
[211] Eron Rowland, *Varina Howell*, pp. 30, 36; Vose, *Southwest Almanac . . . 1836*.

10. Hotel, Parker's.[212] (1836) Situated near the bluff.
11. Hotel.[213] (1836) Fronts on "Cotton Square" and is used by the country people when they bring in their cotton.

Mississippi, general—
1. Tavern, Bishiers.[214] (1807) Located on the Natchez trace near the line that divided the Choctaw Nation from the Mississippi territory.
2. Tavern.[215] (1808) Bruinsbury. One mile below the mouth of bayou Pierre.
3. Two taverns in Greenville.[216] (1808) Greenville, was the capital of Jefferson county; its old name was Huntstown.
4. Three taverns in Sulsertown.[217] (1808) This village contained ten small houses three of which were taverns.
5. Tavern, Hill's.[218] (1808) Washington.
6. Three taverns in Washington.[219] (1808) All of these taverns were on the Natchez road.
7. Hotel, Mickie's.[220] (1808)
8. Tavern, Greaton's.[221] (1808) On the right bank of the Homochito.
9. Tavern, Mrs. Crosby's.[222] (1808)
10. Tavern, Marsalis's.[223] (1808) Fort Adams or Wilkinsonburg.
11. Tavern.[224] (1808) Pinckneyville.
12. Auberge, Madame Le Gendre's.[225] (1808) Baton Rouge.
13. Tavern, Smith's.[226] (1808)
14. Tavern, Trimble's.[227] (1808)
15. Tavern.[228] (1808) Port Gibson.

FLORIDA

Pensacola—
1. Tavern.[229] (1791)

[212] Rowland, *op. cit.*, p. 36. [213] *Ibid.*
[214] Young, *Autobiography of a Pioneer*, p. 215.
[215] Fortescue Cuming, *Sketches of a Tour to the Western Country*, p. 285.
[216] *Ibid.*, pp. 289, 290.
[217] *Ibid.*, pp. 291, 292. [221] *Ibid.*, p. 299. [225] *Ibid.*, pp. 310, 311.
[218] *Ibid.*, p. 292. [222] *Ibid.* [226] *Ibid.*, p. 316.
[219] *Ibid.* [223] *Ibid.*, p. 302. [227] *Ibid.*, p. 319.
[220] *Ibid.*, p. 294. [224] *Ibid.*, p. 303. [228] *Ibid.*, p. 320.
[229] Pope, *op. cit.*, p. 43. Mr. Pope says that in May, 1791 there was only one tavern and its rates were "enormously high."

APPENDIX 157

St. Augustine—
1. The Cottage.[230] (1821) Ann Schelling.
2. Exchange Coffee-House.[231] (1821) Marshall and Ruckman. Opposite the Custom-House.

St. Joseph—
1. Byron House.[232] (1839)
2. Pickwick House.[233] (1839)
3. The Tontine House.[234] (1839) On Jackson at the corner of Palmetto Street.

Tallahassee—
1. Eagle Tavern.[235] (1828) Josiah Everitt.
2. Florida Hotel.[236] (1828) R. K. Call.
3. Planters' Hotel.[237] (1828) William Wyatt.

LOUISIANA

New Orleans—
1. Orleans Hotel.[238] (1788-1842) R. Ruddock. This hotel was built by Mr. Samuel P. Moore about the year 1788 or 1789.
2. Tavern.[239] (1799) Operated by Madam Shaboo.
3. La Maison Coquette.[240] (1802)
4. Tavern.[241] (1804) Operated by Madam Fournier.
5. Le Veau qui Tete.[242] (1805) Corner St. Peter and St. Charles Streets.
6. Strangers' Hotel.[243] (1812-38) R. Marty.

[230] *Florida Gazette*, I (1821), No. 3, included as supplement to J. O. Knauss, *Territorial Florida Journalism*.
[231] *Ibid*.
[232] *St. Joseph Times*, III (1839), No. 17, included as supplement to Knauss, *op. cit*.
[233] *Ibid*.   [234] *Ibid*.
[235] *The Floridian*, I (1828), No. 7, included as supplement to Knauss, *op. cit*. This tavern was formerly occupied by Colonel Geo. Fisher.
[236] *Ibid*.   [237] *Ibid*.
[238] *New Orleans Directory for 1842*, II, 65.
[239] Cuming, *op. cit.*, p. 332.
[240] Berquin-Duvallon, *Travels in Louisiana and the Floridas in the year 1802*, p. 54.
[241] Lathrop, *op. cit.*, p. 234.
[242] *Ibid*.
[243] Featherstonhough, *op. cit.*, II, 262; *New Orleans Directory for 1838*, pp. 330, 331.

7. Cafe des Refugies.[244] (1815)
8. Museum Coffee-House.[245] (1819) Boniface. Opposite the levee.
9. Hotel, Tremoulet's.[246] (1819) On Rue St. Pierre, southwest corner of the square.
10. St. Louis Hotel.[247] (1821-54)
11. Planters' and Merchants' Hotel.[248] (1822) Thomas Beale. 15 Canal Street.
12. Orleans Coffee House.[249] (1824) Luther Morehouse. 83-85 Bienville Street, between Royal and Bourbon Streets.
13. Porter and Oyster House.[250] (1824) Lewis E. Brown. 42 Chartres Street, between Bienville and Custom House Streets.
14. Boarding House.[251] (1828) Operated by Mrs. Herrie.
15. Eastern Hotel.[252] (1831) Robert Carey. Corner of Hospital and Levee Streets.
16. Exchange Hotel.[253] (1835-45) St. Louis Street between Royal and Chartres Streets.
17. Tavern.[254] (1836) Bishop.

[244] Marquis James, *The Raven*, p. 38.
[245] Arthur Singleton, *Letters from the South and West*, pp. 126, 130.
[246] *The Journal of Latrobe*, pp. 164-66, illustration opp. p. 172.
[247] Turnbull, *American Photographs*, II, 31, 32, 45, 46, 47, 55, 56; J. H. Ingraham, *The Sunny South*, pp. 337, 345; Henry A. Murray, *Lands of the Slave and the Free*, pp. 141, 142; Albert Shaw, *Abraham Lincoln*, I, 35; B. M. Norman, *Norman's New Orleans and Environs*, p. 143; A. Oakey Hall, *The Manhattaner in New Orleans*, pp. 17, 18; Theodore Clapp, *Autobiographical Sketches and Recollections during a Thirty-Five Years Residence in New Orleans*, p. 77.
[248] John Adams Paxton, *New Orleans Directory and Register*, p. 18 and advertisement; B. M. Norman, *op. cit.*, p. 143. Before 1822 this hotel was situated at 65 Chartres Street.
[249] John Adams Paxton, *Supplement to the New Orleans Directory of the Last Year* (1824).
[250] *Ibid.*
[251] Mrs. Basil Hall, *op. cit.*, pp. 249, 251, 252, 261.
[252] *Daily Focus* (Louisville, Ky.), I (1831), 220.
[253] Logan, *op. cit.*, p. 180; *New Orleans Directory for 1838*, illustration opp. p. 332; *New Orleans Directory for 1842*, p. 67; Featherstonhaugh, *op. cit.*, II, 262; Norman, *op. cit.*, pp. 157-59, illustration p. 157.
[254] Logan, *op. cit.*, p. 180. According to Mr. Logan this was the best hotel in 1836, and the charges were "very high, being three dollars per day without wine."

APPENDIX   159

18. The Verandah.²⁵⁵ (1838-46) Mr. Meeks. Corner of St. Charles and Common Streets, diagonally opposite the Exchange Hotel. Completed in 1838 and was leased for five years to King and Meeks.
19. Pension Bourgeoise.²⁵⁶ (1841). Mrs. Cohen. 19 Rue Bourbon.
20. National Hotel.²⁵⁷ (1842-45) Tchoupitoulas Street. R. F. Mitchell, John Phillips.
21. Hotel.²⁵⁸ (1845) Hewlett. Corner Camp and Common Streets.
22. St. Charles Hotel.²⁵⁹ (1845-53)

Opelousas—
1. Four Taverns in 1817.²⁶⁰

Franklin, St. Mary's Parish—
1. Two Taverns in 1817.²⁶¹

St. Martinsville—
1. Three Taverns in 1817.²⁶²

²⁵⁵ *New Orleans Directory for 1838*, p. 335, illustration opp. p. 332; *New Orleans Directory for 1842*, pp. 67, 68; A. Oakey Hall, *op. cit.*, p. 16; Norman, *op. cit.*, pp. 141, 142, illustration p. 142.
²⁵⁶ *New Orleans Directory for 1841*, p. 361.
²⁵⁷ *New Orleans Directory for 1842*; Norman, *op. cit.*, p. 143.
²⁵⁸ Norman, *op. cit.*, p. 143.
²⁵⁹ Eron Rowland, *op. cit.*, pp. 106, 107, 111; Mrs. Davis, *Jefferson Davis*, I, 200; Robert Baird, *Impressions and Experiences of the West Indies and North America in 1849*, p. 190; Turnbull, *op. cit.*, II, 55, 56; Stirling, *Letters from the Slave States*, pp. 151, 152, 179, 230; Murray, *op. cit.*, illustration opp. p. 141; A. Oakley Hall, *op. cit.*, pp. 4, 6, 8, 9, 60.
²⁶⁰ *Niles' Weekly Register*, XIII (1817-18), 40.
²⁶¹ *Ibid.*
²⁶² *Ibid.*

BIBLIOGRAPHY

A. Source Material

I. DOCUMENTS

American State Papers; Documents, legislative and executive of the Congresses of the United States, 38 vols., Washington, 1832-1861.

Colonial Records of the State of Georgia, 22 vols., compiled and published under the authority of the legislature by Allen D. Candler, Atlanta, 1904.

Florida Plantation Records, from the papers of George Noble Jones, edited by Ulrich Bonnell Phillips and James David Glaunt. (Publication of the Missouri Historical Society), St. Louis, 1927.

Indian Affairs, Laws and Treaties, 2 vols., compiled and edited by Charles J. Kappler, Washington, 1904.

Mississippi Provincial Archives, 1701-1743, 3 vols., French dominion. Collected, edited, and translated by Dunbar Rowland and A. G. Sanders, Jackson, Mississippi, 1927-1932.

Mississippi Territorial Archives, 1798-1803, Executive Journal of Governor Winthrop Sargent and Governor William Charles Cole Claiborne, compiled and edited by Dunbar Rowland, Nashville, 1905.

"Report on Mail Routes," *Journal of the Continental Congress,* IV, 693, 694.

II. NEWSPAPERS

Alabama Journal (Montgomery), Vol. I (1825)—Vol. VII (1832).

Alexandria Herald, Vol. XII (1821-22).

Cahaba Press and Alabama State Intelligencer, Vol. III (1821-22).

Daily Focus (Louisville), Vol. I (1831).

Georgia Advertiser (Augusta), Vol. III (1821).

Georgia Gazette (Savannah), No. 1 (1763)—No. 346 (1770); name changed to *The Gazette of the State of Georgia,* No. 17

(1783)—No. 299 (1788); name changed again to *The Georgia Gazette,* No. 300 (1788)—No. 361 (1789).
Georgia Journal (Milledgeville), Vols. I. (1810), III (1811).

III. DIRECTORIES

Georgia and South Carolina Almanack, Augusta, 1818.
Georgia and South Carolina Almanack, Augusta, 1820.
Gibson, John, *Gibson's Guide and Directory of the State of Louisiana, and the Cities of New Orleans and Lafayette,* New Orleans, 1838.
James' River Guide: etc., Cincinnati, 1871.
Louisville Directory for the Year 1832, Louisville, 1832.
New Orleans Directory for 1841 (Made by the United States Deputy Marshalls, while taking the late Census), New Orleans, 1840.
New Orleans Directory for 1842, 2 vols. in one, New-Orleans, 1842.
Paxton, John Adams, *The New Orleans Directory and Register.* (One title-page in French and one in English), New Orleans, 1822.
————, *Supplement to the New-Orleans Directory of the Last Year,* New Orleans, 1824.
Sherwood, Adiel, *Gazetteer of the State of Georgia,* Charleston, S. C., 1827.
————, *Gazetteer of the State of Georgia,* 2nd edition, Philadelphia, 1829.
————, *Gazetteer of the State of Georgia,* Washington City, 1837.
Smith and Wooster, *Mississippi and Louisiana Almanac . . . 1833,* Natchez, 1832.
South-Carolina and Georgia Almanac, . . . 1789, Charleston.
South-Carolina and Georgia Almanac, . . . 1798, Charleston.
South-Carolina and Georgia Almanac, . . . 1799, Charleston.
South-Carolina and Georgia Almanac, . . . 1800, Charleston.
Tobler, John, *The South-Carolina and Georgia Almanack, . . . 1765,* Charlestown.

———, *The South-Carolina and Georgia Almanack*, ... *1772*, Charlestown.

———, *The South-Carolina and Georgia Almanack*, ... *1776*, Charlestown.

———, *The South-Carolina and Georgia Almanack*, ... *1781*, Charlestown.

———, *The South-Carolina and Georgia Almanack*, ... *1785*, Charleston.

———, *The South-Carolina and Georgia Almanack*, ... *1786*, Charleston.

———, *The South-Carolina and Georgia Almanac*, ... *1790*, Charleston.

———, *The South-Carolina and Georgia Almanac*, ... *1791*, Charleston.

———, *The South-Carolina and Georgia Almanac*, ... *1792*, Charleston.

Vose, *Mississippi and Louisiana Almanac* ... *1835*, Natchez, 1834.

———, *Southwest Almanac* ... *1836*, Natchez, 1835.

Waring, William, *The South-Carolina and Georgia Almanac,* ... *1793*, Charleston.

IV. GENERAL

Adair, James, *The History of the American Indians;* particularly those Nations adjoining to the Mississippi, East and West Florida, Georgia, South and North Carolina, and Virginia: etc., London, 1775.

Americans as they are; described in a tour through the valley of the Mississippi, by the author of *Austria as it is,* London, 1828.

An Account of the Reception of General Lafayette in Savannah; on Saturday March 19th, 1825, Savannah, 1825.

Arfwedson, C. D., *The United States and Canada, in 1832, 1833, and 1834,* 2 vols., London, 1834.

Audubon, John James, *Delineations of American Scenery and Character,* with an introduction by Francis Hobart Herrick, New York, 1926.

BIBLIOGRAPHY 163

Bartram, William, *Travels through North and South Carolina, East and West Florida, the Cherokee Country, the extensive Territories of the Muscogulges, or Creek Confederacy, and the Country of the Choctaws,* Dublin, 1793.

Bedford, John R. Dr., "A Tour in 1807 down the Cumberland, Ohio, and Mississippi rivers from Nashville to New Orleans," *Tennessee Historical Magazine,* V (1919), 40-68, 107-28.

[Berquin-Duvallon], *Travels in Louisiana and the Floridas in the year 1802,* giving a correct picture of those countries. (Translated from the French of 1802, with notes by John Davis), New York, 1806.

Brackenridge, H. M., *Views of Louisiana, together with a Journal of a voyage up the Missouri River, in 1811,* Pittsburgh, 1814.

Bradbury, John, *Travels in the Interior of America, in the Years 1809, 1810, and 1811;* etc., Liverpool, 1817.

Briggs, Isaac, *Letterbook of Isaac Briggs.*

Bossu, Jean Bernard, *Travels through that Part of North America formerly called Louisiana,* 2 vols., translated from the French by John Reinhold Forster, London, 1771.

"Bourbon county, Georgia, Papers relating to, 1785-1786," edited by Edmund C. Burnett, *American Historical Review,* XV (1910), 66-111, 297-353.

Bourne, Edward Gaylord, *Narratives of the Career of Hernando de Soto,* 2 vols., New York, 1914.

Calles, Christopher, *A Survey of the Roads of the United States of America,* New York, 1789.

(Champigny, Jean Chevalier de), *The Present State of the Country and Inhabitants, Europeans and Indians, of Louisiana,* London, 1744.

Clapp, Theodore, *Autobiographical Sketches and Recollections during a Thirty-Five Years residence in New Orleans,* Boston, 1857.

Collot, Victor, *A Journey in North America,* . . . 2 vols. Translated from the French edition by J. Christian Bay, reprinted from the 1826 Paris edition. (Reprints of Rare Americana, No. 4), Firenze, 1924.

Cramer, Zadok, *The Navigator containing directions for navigating the Monongahela, Allegheny, Ohio, and Mississippi Rivers*, Pittsburgh, 1814, 8th edition. Reprinted in Lechy, *Who's Who on the Ohio*, pp. 83-201.

Cuming, Fortescue, *Sketches of a Tour to the Western Country, through the states of Ohio and Kentucky;* a voyage down the Ohio and Mississippi Rivers, and a trip through the Mississippi Territory, and part of West Florida—commenced at Philadelphia in the winter of 1807, and concluded in 1809, Pittsburgh, 1810.

——————, *Tour to Western Country, . . . 1807-1809*, edited with notes, introduction, etc., by Ruben Gold Thwaites, Cleveland, 1904.

Davis, John, *Travels of John Davis in the United States of America, 1798-1802*, 2 vols., edited by John Vance Cheney, Boston, MDCDX.

Documentary History of American Industrial Society, 10 vols., edited by John R. Commons, Ulrich B. Phillips, Eugene A. Gilmore, Helen L. Sumner, and John B. Andrews, Cleveland, 1910.

Dow, Lorenzo, *History of Cosmopolite; or the four volumes of Lorenzo Dow's Journal concentrated in one*, Washington, Ohio, 1848.

Featherstonhough, G. W., *Excursion through the Slave States*, 2 vols., London, 1844.

Finlay, Hugh, *Journal kept by Hugh Finlay . . . during his Survey of the Post Offices between Falmouth and Casco Bay in the Province of Massachusetts and Savannah in Georgia begun the 13th Sept. 1773 and ended 26th June 1774*, edited by Frank H. Norton, Brooklyn, 1867.

Flint, Timothy, *Recollections of the Last Ten Years passed in occasional residence and journeying in the Valley of the Mississippi*, Boston, 1826.

Forbes, Thomas Semmes, "John Murray Forbes's Horseback Trip to Alabama in 1831," *Alabama Historical Society Transactions*, IV, 445-48.

Gaines, George Strother, "Letters relating to events in South Alabama, 1805-1814," *Alabama Historical Society Transactions*, III, 184-92.
Gallatin, *The Writings of Albert*, 3 vols., edited by Henry Adams, Philadelphia, 1879.
Gillies, John, *Memoirs of Rev. George Whitefield*, Middletown, 1837.
Gist's, Christopher, *Journals*, edited by William M. Darlington, Pittsburgh, 1893.
Grant, James, "Governor James Grant to the Board of Trade, December 1, 1764," *American Historical Review*, XX (1915), 827-31.
Hall, A. Oakey, *The Manhattaner in New Orleans, or, Phases of "Crescent City" Life*, New York, 1851.
Hall, Captain Basil, *Forty Etchings*, from sketches made with the Camera Lucida, in North America, in 1827 and 1828, Edinburgh and London, 1829.
Hall, Mrs. Basil, *The Aristocratic Journey*, being the Outspoken letters of Mrs. Basil Hall written during a Fourteen Months Sojourn in America 1827-1828, prefaced and edited by Una Pope-Hennessy, New York, 1931.
Hall, James, *Notes on Western States, descriptive sketches of soil, climate, resources, and scenery*, Philadelphia, 1838.
Hamilton, Thomas, *Men and Manners in America*, London and Edinburgh, 1843.
"Hawkins, Letters of Benjamin, 1796-1806," *Collections of the Georgia Historical Society*, IX (1916).
Hodgson, Adam, *Letters from North America*, written during a tour in the United States and Canada, 2 vols., London, 1824.
Imlay, Gilbert, *A Description of the Western Territory of North America; etc.*, Dublin, 1793.
Jefferys, Thomas, *The American Atlas: or, a geographical description of the whole continent of America*, London, 1776.
Johnson, William, "William Johnson's Journal," introduction by Henry P. Dart, *Louisiana Historical Quarterly*, V (1922), 34-50. Also found in *New Jersey Quarterly Magazine*, Jan. and April, 1922.

Ker, Henry, *Travels through the Western Interior of the United States, from the year 1808 up to the year 1816* . . . , Elizabethtown, N. J., 1816.

Kolm, Peter, *Travels into North America,* 3 vols., translated into English by John Reinhold Forster, London, 1771.

Lara, Jose Bernardo Gutierrez de, "Diary of Jose Bernardo Gutierrez de Lara," Part I (Nov. 2, 1811-Dec. 31, 1811), edited by Elizabeth Howard West, *American Historical Review,* XXXIV (1928-29), 55-77.

Latrobe, Benjamin H., *The Journal of Latrobe,* . . . *1796-1820,* introduction by J. H. B. Latrobe, New York, 1905.

Latrobe, Charles Joseph, *The Rambler in North America, 1832-1833,* 2 vols., 2nd edition, London, 1836.

Levasseur, A., *Lafayette in America in 1824 and 1825 or Journal of a Voyage to the United States,* 2 vols., translated by John D. Godman, Philadelphia, 1829.

Lincecum, Gideon, "Autobiography of Gideon Lincecum," *Mississippi Historical Society Publications,* VIII (1904), 433-519.

Lisbomb, A. A., *North and South Impressions of Northern Society by a Southerner,* Mobile, 1853.

Logan, James, *Notes of a Journey through Canada, the United States of America, and the West Indies,* Edinburgh, 1838.

Luna Papers, 2 vols., documents relating to the Expedition of Don Tristán de Luna y Arellano for the conquest of La Florida in 1559-1561, translated and edited by Herbert Ingram Priestley. (Publication of the Florida State Historical Society, No. 8), Deland, Florida, 1928.

Magruder, Allan B., *A Letter from Allan B. Magruder, Esq. of Opelousas, to his Correspondent in the State of Virginia, Dated 20th Nov. 1807,* New Orleans, 1808.

Melish, John, *Description of the Roads in the United States,* Philadelphia, 1814.

⸻, *Travels through the United States of America,* in the years 1806 & 1807, and 1809, 1810, & 1811; etc., Belfast, 1818.

Men and Manners in America, 2 vols., by the author of *Cyril Thornton, Esq.,* Philadelphia, 1833.

Milfort, Le Gal, *Mémoire ou coup-d'oeil rapide sur mes différens voyages et mon séjour dans la nation Crëck*, Paris, 1802.

Moore, Francis, *A Voyage to Georgia, begun in the year 1735*, London, 1744.

"Narrative of Alvar Nuñez Cabeça de Vaca" (*in Spanish Explorers in the Southern United States, 1528-1543*), edited by Frederick W. Hodge, New York, 1907.

"The Narrative of the Expedition of Hernando de Soto by the Gentleman of Elvas" (in *Spanish Explorers in the Southern United States, 1528-1543*), edited by Theodore H. Lewis, New York, 1907.

Official Letter Books of W. C. C. Claiborne, 1801-1816, 6 vols., edited by Dunbar Rowland, Jackson, Mississippi, 1917.

Owen, John, "John Owen's Journal of his removal from Virginia to Alabama in 1818," *Publications Southern History Association*, I (1897), 89-97.

"Pages from a Journal of a voyage down the Mississippi to New Orleans in 1817," edited by Felix Flugal, *Louisiana Historical Quarterly*, VII (1924), 414-40.

Perrin-du-Lac, François M., *Voyage dans Les deux Louisianes, et chez Les Nations Sauvages du Missouri, ... en 1801, 1802, et 1803; ...*, Paris, 1805.

Philips, Martin W., "Diary of a Mississippi planter, January 1, 1840, to April, 1863," edited by Franklin L. Riley, *Mississippi Historical Society Publications*, X (1909), 305-481.

Pittman, Captain Philips, *The Present State of the European Settlement on the Mississippi with a geographical description of that river*, exact reprint of the original edition, London, 1770, with introduction, notes, etc., by Frank Heywood Hodder, Cleveland, 1906.

Pope, John, *A Tour through the Southern and Western Territories of the United States of North America; the Spanish Dominions on the river Mississippi and the Floridas; the countries of the Creek Nations; and many uninhabited parts*, Richmond, 1792.

Rochefoucauld-Liancourt, La, *Voyage dans les États-Unis d' Amérique, fait en 1795, 1796 et 1797*, 8 vols., Paris, L'an VII.

Schoepf, Johann David, *Travels in the Confederation (1783-1784)*, 2 vols., translated and edited by Alfred J. Morrison, Philadelphia, 1911.

Schultz, Christian, Jun., *Travels on an Inland Voyage through the States of New-York, Pennsylvania, Virginia, Ohio, Kentucky and Tennessee*, . . . *in the years 1807 and 1808*, 2 vols. in one, New York, 1810.

Smyth, J. F. D., *A Tour in the United States of America;* containing an account of the present situation of that country; . . . with a description of the Indian nations, . . . 2 vols., London, 1784.

Sparks, William Henry, *The Memories of Fifty Years*, Philadelphia, 1870.

Stirling, James, *Letters from the Slave States*, London, 1857.

Stork, William, ed., *A Description of East Florida*, with a Journal, kept by John Bartram of Philadelphia, . . . 3rd edition, London, 1769.

————, ed., *An Account of East Florida*, with remarks on its future Importance to Trade and Commerce, London, (1766).

Stuart, John, "Observations on the Plan for the Future Management of the Indian Affairs Humbly submitted to the Lords Commissioners of Trade and Plantations," *American Historical Review*, XX (1915), 817-27.

Turnbull, Jane M. C. and Marion, *American Photographs*, 2 vols., London, 1859.

Volney, C. F., *View of the Climate and Soil of the United States of America*, London, 1804.

Warden, D. B., *Statistical, Political, and Historical Account of the United States of North America*, 3 vols., Edinburgh, 1819.

Washington, George, *Letters and Recollections of George Washington*, New York, 1906.

————, *The Diaries of George Washington 1748-1799*, 4 vols., edited by John C. F. Fitzpatrick, New York, 1925.

Watson, Elkanah, *Men and Times of the Revolution;* or Memoirs of Elkanah Watson, including his Journals of Travels in

Europe and America, from the year 1777 to 1842, edited by his son Winslow C. Watson, 2nd edition, New York, 1857.

Weld, Isaac, Junior, *Travels through the States of North America, and the Provinces of Upper and Lower Canada, during the years 1795, 1796, and 1797,* London, 1799.

Wills, William Henry, "A Southern Sulky Ride in 1837, from North Carolina to Alabama," *Publications Southern Historical Association,* VI (1902), 471-483, VII (1903), 7-17, 79-85, 187-93.

———, "A Southern Traveler's Diary in 1840," *Publications Southern Historical Association,* VII (1903), 349-52, 427-33; VIII (1904), 23-40, 129-39.

B. SECONDARY MATERIAL

I. GENERAL

Abernethy, Thomas Perkins, *The Formative Period in Alabama, 1815-1828* (Publication of the Alabama State Department of Archives and History, History and Patriotic Series, No. 6), Montgomery, Alabama, 1922.

[Armroyd, George], *A Connected View of the Whole Internal Navigation of the United States, Natural and Artificial; Present and Prospective,* Philadelphia, 1826.

Audubon, Life and Adventures of, The Naturalist, edited by Robert Buchanan, introduction by John Burroughs. (Everyman's Library Series), London, n. d.

Bassett, J. S., *The Southern Plantation Overseer,* Northampton, Mass., 1925.

Betts, E. C., *Early History of Huntsville, Alabama,* Montgomery, 1909.

Brannon, Peter A., *Highway Boats and Bridges,* Montgomery, 1929.

———, *Historic Highways in Alabama,* Montgomery, 1929.

Brevard, Caroline Mays, *A History of Florida* from the treaty of 1763 to our own time, 2 vols., edited by James Alexander Robertson. (Publication of the Florida State History Association, No. 4), Deland, Florida, 1924.

Chambers, Henry E., *Mississippi Valley Beginnings,* New York, 1922.
Darby, William, *A Geographical Description of the State of Louisiana, the Southern part of the State of Mississippi, and Territory of Alabama,* 2nd edition, New York, 1817.
————, *The Emigrant's Guide to the Western and Southwestern States and Territories,* New York, 1818.
Davis, Ruben, *Recollections of Mississippi and Mississippians,* New York, 1891.
Dunbar, Seymour, *A History of Travel in America,* 4 vols., Indianapolis, (1915).
Durrenberger, Joseph Austin, *Turnpikes,* Valdosta, Ga., 1931.
Eighty Years' Progress of the United States, 2 vols., New York, 1861.
Filson, John, *The Discovery, Settlement and Present State of Kentucke,* Wilmington, 1784. Reprinted in Louisville, 1930.
Finley, John, *The French in the Heart of America,* New York, 1915.
Flint, Timothy, *Condensed Geography and History of the Western States, or the Mississippi Valley,* 2 vols., Cincinnati, 1828.
Fortier, Alcée, *Louisiana;* comprising sketches of countries, towns, events, institutions, and persons, arranged in cyclopedic form, 2 vols. and a supplementary volume of contemporary biography, Atlanta, 1909.
Gamble, Thomas, *Savannah Duels and Duellists, 1733-1877,* Savannah, 1923.
Gayarré, Charles E. A., *History of Louisiana,* 4 vols. (vols. I, II, "French Domination," vol. III, "Spanish Domination," vol. IV, "American Domination"), 3rd edition enlarged, New Orleans, 1885.
Gephart, William Franklin, *Transportation and Industrial Development in the Middle West* (Columbia University Studies in History, Economics, and Public Law, vol. XXXIV, no. 1), New York, 1909.
Gillespie, W. M., *A Manual of Principles and Practice of Road-Making,* New York, 1853.

[Gilmer, George R., Governor], *Sketches of some of the First Settlers of Upper Georgia, of the Cherokees, and the Author,* Americus, Georgia, 1926.
Greene, Evarts Boutell, *Provincial America, 1690-1704* (American Nation Series, volume 6), New York, 1905.
Gregg, Wm., *Essay on Plank Roads,* Charleston, S. C., 1851.
Hamilton, Peter J., *Colonial Mobile,* New York, 1910.
Harlow, Alvin F., *Old Post Bags,* The Story of the Sending of a Letter in Ancient and Modern Times, New York, 1928.
Henderson, Archibald, *Washington's Southern Tour 1791,* Boston and New York, 1923.
Heustis, Jabez W., *Physical Observations, and Medical Tracts and Researches, on the Topography and Diseases of Louisiana,* New York, 1817.
Houghton, G. W. W., *The Hub's Vocabulary of Vehicles,* New York, 1892.
Hulbert, Archer B., *Historical Highways of America,* 16 vols., Cleveland, 1902-1905.
―――――, *The Paths of Inland Commerce,* A Chronicle of Trail, Road and Waterway (Yale Chronicle Series), New Haven, 1920.
Hutchins, Thomas, *An Historical Narrative and Topographical Description of Louisiana, and West-Florida,* Philadelphia, 1784.
Jones, Charles Colcock, Jr., *History of Georgia,* 2 vols., Boston, 1883.
―――――, *Memorial History of Augusta, Georgia,* from the close of the 18th Century, by Salem Dutcher, Syracuse, New York, 1890.
Kingsford, W., *History, Structure, and Statistics of Plank Roads,* Philadelphia, 1851.
Kirkpatrick, John Ervin, *Timothy Flint, Pioneer, Missionary, Author, Editor, 1780-1840,* Cleveland, 1911.
Konwiser, Harry Myron, *Colonial and Revolutionary Posts,* Richmond, Va., 1931.
Knauss, James Owen, *Territorial Florida Journalism,* Deland, Florida, 1926.

Lathrop, Elise, *Early American Inns and Taverns,* New York, 1926.
Leahy, Ethel C., *Who's Who on the Ohio River and its Tributaries,* Cincinnati, 1931.
Lee, F. D. and Agnew, J. L., *Historical Record of the City of Savannah,* Savannah, 1869.
Leech, Daniel D. T., *The Post Office Department,* Washington, D. C., 1879.
Lipscomb, W. L., *A History of Columbus, Mississippi during the 19th Century,* 1909.
Lowery, Woodbury, *The Spanish Settlements within the present Limits of the United States, 1513-1561,* New York, 1901.
M'Call, Hugh, Captain, *The History of Georgia,* 1st edition, vol. I (1811), vol. II (1816). Reprinted Atlanta, 1909.
MacDonald, Thos. H., "Fifty Years of Progress in Highway Improvement in Southern States," *The South's Development,* Baltimore, 1924.
――――――, *History and Development of Road Building in the United States,* Washington, 1926.
――――――, *Two Thousand Years of Road Building,* Washington, 1927.
MacGill, Caroline E., *History of Transportation in the United States before 1860,* prepared under the direction of Balthasar Henry Meyer by Caroline E. MacGill and a Staff of Collaborators, Washington, 1917.
Marshall, Humphrey, *The History of Kentucky,* 2 vols., Frankfort, Kentucky, 1812.
Martin, Francis Xavier, *History of Louisiana from earliest period,* 2 vols., New Orleans, 1827-29.
Martin, John H., *Columbus, Georgia,* from its selection as a "Trading Town" in 1827 to its Partial Destruction by Wilson's Raid in 1865, Columbus, Georgia, 1874.
Martin, William Elejius, *Internal Improvements in Alabama* (Johns Hopkins University Studies, Series 20, No. 4), Baltimore, 1902.
Maynard, Theodore, *De Soto and the Conquistadores,* New York, 1930.

Melius, Louis, *The American Postal Service*, 2nd edition, Washington, (1917).
Mell, P. H., Jr., *Life of Patrick Hues Mell*, Louisville, Kentucky, 1895.
Mesick, Jane Louise, *The English Traveller in America 1785-1835*, New York, 1922.
Monette, John W., *History of the Discovery and Settlement of the Valley of the Mississippi* by the three great European powers, Spain, France, and Great Britain; the subsequent occupation, settlement, and extension of civil government by the United States until 1846, 2 vols., New York, 1846.
Morse, Jedidiah, *American Gazetteer,* civil divisions, rivers, harbors, Indian tribes, etc., Boston, 1810.
————, and Morse, R. C., *Travelers' Guide, or a pocket gazetter of the United States,* New Haven, 1826.
Nevins, Allen (ed. and comp.), *American Social History as recorded by British Travellers,* New York, 1923.
Norman, B. M., *Norman's New Orleans and Environs,* New Orleans, 1845.
Omwake, John, *The Conestoga Six-Horse Bell Teams,* Cincinnati, 1930.
Phillips, Ulrich Bonnell, *American Negro Slavery,* A survey of the supply, employment, and control of negro labor as determined by the Plantation régime, New York, 1928.
————, *History of Transportation in the Eastern Cotton Belt to 1860,* New York, 1908.
————, *Plantation and Frontier Documents: 1649-1864,* 2 vols., Cleveland, 1910.
Pickett, Albert James, *History of Alabama and incidently of Georgia and Mississippi from the earliest period,* Charleston, 1851.
Rich, Wesley Everett, *The History of the United States Post Office to the Year 1829* (Harvard Economic Studies, vol. XXVII), Cambridge, 1924.
Ringwalt, J. L., *Development of the Transportation Systems of the United States,* Philadelphia, 1888.

Roper, Daniel C., *The United States Post Office,* New York, 1917.
Rowland, Dunbar, *History of Mississippi, the Heart of the South,* 2 vols., Chicago, 1925.
Rowland, Eron Opha, "Mrs. Dunbar Rowland," *Varina Howell, Wife of Jefferson Davis,* New York, vol. I, 1927, vol. II, 1931.
St. Clair, Labert, *Since Time began Transportation—Land, Air, Water,* New York, 1933.
Saunders, James Edmonds, *Early Settlers of Alabama,* New Orleans, 1899.
Schouler, James, *Americans of 1776,* New York, 1906.
Semple, Ellen Churchill, *American History and its Geographical Conditions,* Boston and New York, 1903.
Seybert, Adam, *Annales Statistiques des États-Unis,* Paris, 1820.
Sibbald, George, *Notes and Observations, on the Pine Lands of Georgia,* Augusta, 1801. Reprinted as Extra Number (No. 57) of the *Magazine of History,* 1917.
Spafford, Horatio Gates, *Some Cursory Observations on the Ordinary Construction of Wheel-carriages,* Albany, 1815.
Stratton, Ezra M., *The World on Wheels; or Carriages,* New York, 1878.
Surrey, N. M. Miller, *The Commerce of Louisiana during the French Régime, 1699-1763* (Columbia University Studies in History, Economics, and Public Law, LXXI, no. 1), New York, 1916.
Swanton, John R., *Early History of the Creek Indians and their Neighbors* (Bureau of American Ethnology, bulletin 73), Washington, 1922.
————, *Indian Tribes of the Lower Mississippi Valley* (Bureau of American Ethnology, bulletin 43), Washington, 1911.
Turner, Frederick Jackson, *The Frontier in American History,* New York, 1920.
Wade, John Donald, *Augustus Baldwin Longstreet;* a study of the development of culture in the South, New York, 1924.
Whitaker, Arthur Preston, *The Spanish-American Frontier: 1783-1795,* Boston and New York, 1927.
Williamson, Jefferson, *The American Hotel; an anecdotal history,* New York, 1930.

Wilson, Adelaide, *Historic and Picturesque Savannah,* Boston, 1889.

Woods, Michael Leonard, *Personal Reminiscences of Colonel Albert James Pickett,* Montgomery, Alabama, 1904. (Reprint no. 27 from *Alabama Historical Society Transactions,* vol. IV.)

Wright, Richardson, *Hawkers & Walkers in Early America; Strolling Peddlers, Preachers, Lawyers, Doctors, Players, and others from the beginning to the Civil War,* Philadelphia, 1927.

II. PERIODICALS

Adams, Ephraim Douglas, "The Point of View of the British Traveller in America," *Political Science Quarterly,* XXIX (1914), 244-64.

Armstrong, Emma Kate, "Chateaubriand's America. Arrival in America and First Impressions," *Publications of the Modern Language Association of America,* XXII (1907), 345-70.

Bakewell, Gordon, "Reminiscences of John James Audubon," *Publications of the Louisiana Historical Society,* V (1911), 31-41.

Ballagh, James Curtis, "Southern economic history: Tariff and Public land," *American Historical Association Report,* 1898, pp. 223-63.

Berry, Jane M., "Spanish and American Indian Policy, 1783-1795," *Mississippi Valley Historical Review,* III (1916-17), 462-77.

Brannon, Peter A., "Federal Road, Alabama's First Improved Highway," *Alabama Highways,* I (1927), No. 2 (May), 7-10, 19.

————, "Post Roads and Stage Coach Travel in Early Days," *Alabama Highways,* I (1927), 3, 5-6.

————, "Three Notch Road," *Alabama Highways,* I (1927), No. 4 (July), 3, 5, 7-8.

————, "Three Notch Road," *Arrow Points,* VII (1923), 35-38.

————, "Two Centuries of Travel and Transportation," *Alabama Highways,* IV (1930), No. 8 (Nov.), 3, 5-9.

Brets, Julian P., "Early Land Communication with the Lower Mississippi Valley," *Mississippi Valley Historical Review*, XIII (1926), 1-29.

Callendar, G. S., "Early Transportation and Banking Enterprises of the States in Relation to the Growth of Corporations," *Quarterly Journal of Economics*, XVII (1902-1903), 111-62.

Carson, W. Wallace, "Transportation and Traffic on the Ohio and Mississippi before the Steamboat," *Mississippi Valley Historical Review*, VII (1920-21), 26-38.

Carter, Clarence E., "Some Aspects of British Administration in West Florida," *Mississippi Valley Historical Review*, I (1914), 364-75. (Original in the Public Record Office: Colonial Office, 5.585.)

Chambers, Henry E., "Early Commercial Prestige of New Orleans," *Louisiana Historical Quarterly*, V (1922), 451-61.

"Contemporary English view on the trade and prospects of New Orleans at the close of the French dominion," Extract from "Observation on West Florida" by Jacob Blackwell, about 1766 (from the *Shelburne Papers*, XLVIII, 19-27), *Louisiana Historical Quarterly*, VI (1923), 221-22.

Cotterill, R. S., "The Beginnings of Railroads in the Southwest," *Mississippi Valley Historical Review*, VIII (1922), 318-27.

————, "The Natchez Trace," *Tennessee Historical Magazine*, VII (1921), 27-35. Reprinted in *Louisiana Historical Quarterly*, VI (1922), 259-68.

————, "The National Land System in the South: 1803-1812," *Mississippi Valley Historical Review*, XVI (1930), 495-506.

Crane, Verner W., "The Southern Frontier in Queen Anne's War," *American Historical Review*, XXIV (1919), 379-95.

————, "The Tennessee River as the Road to Carolina: the beginnings of exploration and trade," *Mississippi Valley Historical Review*, III (1916-17), 3-18.

Dart, Henry P., "A Louisiana Indigo Plantation on Bayou Teche, 1773," text translated by Laura L. Porteous, *Louisiana Historical Quarterly*, IX (1925), 565-90.

————, "Episodes of Life in Colonial Louisiana," *Louisiana Historical Quarterly*, VI (1923), 35-45.

"Development of Highway Transportation," *Tennessee Highway and Public Works*, V (1926), No. 1 (June), 18-19; No. 2 (Sept.), 12-13.

Dozier, Howard Douglas, "Trade and Transportation along the South Atlantic Seaboard before the Civil War," *South Atlantic Quarterly*, XVIII (1919), 231-45.

Edwards, L. N. (Capt.), "Early American Bridges" (Résumé of paper on "The Evolution of Early American Bridges"), *Engineering*, 135 (1933), 389-90.

Emerson, Frederick V., "Geographic Influences in the Mississippi Valley," *Mississippi Valley Historical Association Proceedings*, VIII (1914-15), 289-96.

"Evolution of a Road from Indian Trail to Modern Highway," *Road Economics*, V (1924), No. 10 (April), 9-12.

Few, William, "Autobiography of Colonel William Few of Georgia," *Magazine of American History*, VII (1881), 334 ff.

Fitzpatrick, John C., "The Post Office of the Revolutionary," *Daughters of the American Revolution Magazine*, LVI (1922), 575-88.

Galloway, Charles B. (Bishop), "Lorenzo Dow in Mississippi," *Publications Mississippi Historical Society*, IV (1900), 233-44.

Galpin, W. F., "The Grain Trade of New Orleans, 1804-1814," *Mississippi Valley Historical Review*, XIV (1927), 496-507.

Gayarré, Charles, "Historical Notes on the Commerce and Agriculture of Louisiana, 1720-1766," *Louisiana Historical Quarterly*, II (1918), 286-91.

Gonzalez, S. J. (Mrs.), "Pensacola; its early history," *Florida Historical Society Quarterly*, II (1909), 9-25.

Grant, Ludovick, "Historical relations of facts delivered by Ludovick Grant, Indian trader, to his excellency the Governor of South Carolina," *South Carolina Historical Magazine*, X (1909), 54-68.

Halbert, H. S., "Choctaw Crossing Places on the Tombigbee," *Publications Alabama Historical Society*, I (1909), 430-31.

Hamer, Philip M., "John Stuart's Indian Policy during the early months of the American Revolution," *Mississippi Valley Historical Review*, XVII (1930), 351-66.

———, "The British in Canada and the Southern Indians, 1790-1794," *East Tennessee Historical Society Publications*, II (1930), 107-34.

Hamilton, Peter J., "Early Roads of Alabama," *Alabama Historical Society Transactions*, II (1897), 39-56.

———, "Indian Trails and Early Roads," *Alabama Historical Society Transactions*, I (1896), 422-29.

———, "St. Stephens; Spanish Fort and American Town," *Alabama Historical Society Transactions*, III (1898), 227-34.

———, "The Beginnings of French Settlement of the Mississippi Valley," *Gulf States Historical Magazine*, I (1902), 1-12.

Harper, Roland M., "Some Relations between soil, climate, and civilization in the Southern Red Hills of Alabama," *South Atlantic Quarterly*, XIX (1920), 201-15.

Harrison, Fairfax, "The Virginians on the Ohio and the Mississippi in 1742," *Louisiana Historical Quarterly*, V (1922), 316-332; also in *Virginia Magazine of History and Biography*, XXX (1922), 203-22.

Hawkins, H. G., "History of Port Gibson, Mississippi," *Mississippi Historical Society Publications*, X (1909), 279-99.

Henderson, Archibald, "The Beginnings of American Expansion," *North Carolina Review*, I (1910), 1 ff.; II (1910), 15 ff.

Hubbard, George D., "Geographic Factors in the Economic Progress of the South," *Bulletin of the Geographical Society of Philadelphia*, XVII (1919), 131-37.

Hulbert, Archer B., "The Indian Thoroughfares," *Ohio Archaeological and Historical Society Publications*, VIII (1900), 264-95.

Johnson, Emory R., "Geographical Influences Affecting the Early Development of American Commerce," *Bulletin American Geographical Society*, XL (1908), 129-43.

Jones, Charles C., Jr., "Dead Towns of Georgia," *Georgia Historical Society Collections*, IV (1878).

Jones, J. II., "Evolution of Wilkinson County," *Mississippi Historical Society Publications*, XI (1910), 75-85.

Keene, Otis L., "Jacksonville Fifty-Three Years Ago," *Florida Historical Society Quarterly,* I (1909), 9-15.
Kelly, H. H., "Toll Roads," *Public Roads,* XII (1931), 1-10.
Kerr, C. M., "Highway Progress in Louisiana," *Louisiana Historical Quarterly,* vol. II (1918), pt. I, pp. 56-71.
Kohl, J. G., "Substance of a lecture delivered at the Smithsonian Institute on the collection of Charts and Maps of America," *Annual Report, Smithsonian Institute,* 1856, pp. 93-146.
Laurent, Lubin F., "History of St. John the Baptist Parish," *Louisiana Historical Quarterly,* VII (1924), 316-31.
Lee, Umphrey, "John Wesley in Arcadia," *Southwest Review,* XIII (1928), 413-32.
Leftwich, George J., "Colonel George Strother Gaines and others, Pioneers in Mississippi Territory," *Mississippi Historical Society Publications,* Centenary Series, I (1916), 442-56.
―――――, "Cotton Gin Port and Gaines' Trace," *Mississippi Historical Society Publications,* VII (1903), 263-70.
―――――, "Some Main Travelled Roads, including cross sections of Natchez trace," *Mississippi Historical Society Publications,* Centenary Series, I (1916), 463-76.
Lippincott, Isaac, "Internal Trade of the United States, 1700-1860," *Washington University Studies,* vol. IV, pt. II, no. 1 (1916), pp. 63-150.
Love, William A., "General Jackson's Military Road," *Mississippi Historical Society Publications,* XI (1905), 403-17.
―――――, "Route of De Soto's expedition through Lowndes County, Mississippi," *Mississippi Historical Society Publications,* IV (1921), 268-76.
Mathews, Maxine, "Old Inns of East Tennessee," *East Tennessee Historical Society Publications,* II (1930), 22-33.
Myer, William E., "Indian Trails of the Southeast," *42nd Annual Report, Bureau American Ethnology,* 1924-25, pp. 729-857.
"New Orleans and Bayou St. John in 1766, Extract from Journal of an expedition along the Ohio and Mississippi by Captain Harry Gordon, 1766, Shelburne MMS, XLVIII, 159-78, *Louisiana Historical Quarterly,* VI (1923), 19, 20.

"New Orleans in 1758"; being the experiences of William Perry, an American Seaman, held in "Jayl" there as a French Prisoner of war, *Louisiana Historical Quarterly,* V (1922), 53-57.

Phillips, Ulrich Bonnell, "Early Railroads in Alabama," *Gulf States Historical Magazine,* I (1902), 345-47.

―――――, "Historical Notes of Milledgeville, Georgia," *Gulf States Historical Magazine,* II (1903), 161-71.

Pilcher, Joe Mitchell, "The Story of Marksville, La.," *Louisiana Historical Society Publications,* X (1918), 68-86.

Reed, Susan Martha, "British Cartography of the Mississippi Valley in the Eighteenth Century," *Mississippi Valley Historical Review,* II (1915), 213-24.

Renshaw, Henry, "Lafayette's Visit to New Orleans," *Louisiana Historical Quarterly,* vol. I (1917), pt. 2, pp. 5-8.

Renshaw, James A., "Lafayette, His Visit to New Orleans in 1825," *Louisiana Historical Quarterly,* IX (1926), 182-90.

Riley, Franklin L., "Extinct Towns and Villages of Mississippi," *Mississippi Historical Society Publications,* V (1901), 311-83.

Rothrock, Mary V., "Carolina Traders among the over-hill Cherokees, 1690-1760," *East Tennessee Historical Society Publications,* I (1929), 3-18.

Royce, Charles C., "Indian Land Cessions in the United States," *18th Annual Report, Bureau American Ethnology,* 1896, pt. 2.

Sandoz, William J., "A Brief History of St. Landry Parish," *Louisiana Historical Quarterly,* VIII (1925), 221-39.

Scroggs, William O., "Early Trade and Travel in the Lower Mississippi Valley," *Mississippi Valley Historical Association Proceedings,* II (1909), 235-56.

―――――, "Rural Life in the Lower Mississippi Valley about 1803," *Mississippi Valley Historical Association Proceedings,* VIII (1914-15), 262-77.

Siebert, Wilbur H., "The Loyalists in West Florida and the Natchez District," *Mississippi Valley Historical Association Proceedings,* VIII (1914-15), 102-22.

Sergeant, V. Heber, "The First Roads of All," *The Highway Magazine,* vol. XXIII (1932), no. 3 (March), pp. 63-65.

Swanton, John R., "Social and Religious Beliefs and Usages of the Chickasaw Indians," *44th Annual Report, Bureau American Ethnology*, 1926-27, pp. 169-275.

Turner, Frederick Jackson, "The Significance of the Frontier," *Annual Report, American Historical Association*, 1893, pp. 197-227.

————, "The Old West," *Wisconsin Historical Society Proceedings*, LVI (1909), 184-233.

Verable, W. H., "Down South before the war, Record of a ramble to New Orleans in 1858," *Ohio Archaeological and Historical Society Publications*, II (1888), 461-84.

Villiers, Baron Marc de, "A History of the Foundation of New Orleans," translated from French by Warrington Dawson, *Louisiana Historical Quarterly*, III (1919), 157-251.

————, "Documents concerning the history of the Indians of the Eastern region of Louisiana," extract from "Journal de la Société des Américanistes de Paris," n. s. XIV (1922), 127-40; *Louisiana Historical Quarterly*, VIII (1925), 28-40.

Welsh, Mary J., "Recollections of Pioneer Life in Mississippi." *Mississippi Historical Society Publications*, IV (1901), 343-56.

Whitaker, Arthur Preston, "The Commerce of Louisiana and the Floridas at the End of the Eighteenth Century," *Hispanic American Historical Review*, VIII (1928), 190-203.

Whitfield, Gaius, Jr., "The French Grant in Alabama," *Alabama Historical Society Transactions*, IV (1899), 321-35.

————, "The French Grant in Alabama, a History of the Founding of Demopolis," *Alabama Polytechnic Institute Historical Papers*, 1st series (1904), pp. 137-63.

Wilkinson, James, "General James Wilkinson," *Louisiana Historical Quarterly*, vol. I (1917), pt. 2, pp. 79-166.

Winston, James E., "Notes on the Economic History of New Orleans, 1803-1836," *Mississippi Valley Historical Review*, XI (1924), 200-226.

Woolley, Mary E., "Early History of the Colonial Post Office," *Rhode Island Historical Society Publications*, I (1894), 270-91.

Zacharie, James S., "New Orleans—Its Old Streets and Places," *Louisiana Historical Society Publications*, vol. II (1918), pt. 3, pp. 45-88.

INDEX

ABINGDON, 78.
Adair, James, 6; description of method employed in crossing deep rivers, 13.
Adams, Ephraim Douglas, 37.
Alabama, 65, 87, 90, 97, 116, 130; termination of Alleghany Mountains in northern, 3; Indian inhabitants, 7; emigrants in, 40, 41, 80, 85; mail destined to, 68.
Alabama River, 3, 4, 7, 17, 26, 28, 56, 59, 64, 84, 86, 89, 128.
Alleghany Mountains, 84; termination of, 3.
Altamaha River, 4, 42, 46, 121, 125.
Apalachicola, 62.
Apalachicola River, 4.
Appalachian Mountains, 13, 38, 52, 79, 117, 138; as a barrier to direct east and west communication, 51.
Arfwedson, Carl, 95.
Ashley Ferry, 126.
Athens (Ga.), 57, 64, 68, 94.
Atkins, Edmond, 23.
Audubon, John James, 40, 41, 68.
Augusta (Ga.), 24, 42, 78, 90, 95, 101, 119; on the fall line, 3; travel to, from Savannah, Georgia, 4; path from Savannah to, 20, 21; as trading center, 20, 21; settlement, 21; road from Savannah to, 47-49, 79, 80; value of, as trading center, 48; paths radiating from, 48; distributing office for mail, 69; path from, to New Orleans, 79; path from, to Mobile, 81, 82; bridge at, 119 ff.; ferry at, 123.
Austin, Stephen F., 65.

BAILY, Francis, 99.
Baker, Isaac L., 65.
Baltimore (Md.), 66.
Barbour, James, Secretary of War, 77.
Barge, 11.

Barnwell's Bluff, path from, to Savannah, 42, 121.
Barry, Postmaster General, 78.
Barter trade, 8.
Bartram, William, 7, 18, 117.
Baton Rouge (La.), 60; stage between New Orleans and, 91.
Bayou Catherine, 60.
Bays—
  Biloxi, 56.
  Mobile, 4, 26, 84, 86.
  St. Louis, 56.
  Tampa, 14.
Bell, Charles, letter from R. J. Meigs to, 67.
Benton, Thomas Hart, 5.
Bernard, S., General, 74, 76, 77.
Berquin-Duvallon, 93, 127.
Bibb, William W., Governor, 87, 116.
Biedma, 10.
Biloxi Bay, 56.
Blakely (Ala.), 86; ferry between Mobile and, 128.
Boats, 48.
  barge, 11.
  canoe, 13, 125, 127.
  "dug-out," 10.
  ferry, 14, 119 ff.
  flats, 126.
  piragua, 10.
  raft, 11.
  skows, 126.
Bolivar Indian Trail, 89.
Brewton, Miles, 123.
Brian Creek, 124.
Bridge, 122; Indian, 9; Spanish, 10; need of, 43, 46, 87; repair of, 59, 127; condition of Indian, 88; improvement of, 117 ff.; "raccoon," 117.
Briggs, Isaac, 65; Jefferson's discussion of mail route with, 52; offer to make preliminary survey, 53; letter to Jefferson (Sept. 2, 1804), 53, 54;

[183]

184 INDEX

letter to Jefferson (Oct. 1804), 54, 55; letter to Jefferson (Nov. 26, 1804), 56, 57; report of survey, 57 ff.; letter from Jefferson (May 25, 1807), 60; petition presented to House of Representatives, 61.
Browne, Montfort, 91.
Burt and Stebbins, 109.
Byrd, Edward, 109.

CAHAWBA *Press*, 69.
Cahawba River, 80.
Calfrey, Lewis, 89.
Calhoun, J. C., Secretary of War, 41, 73.
Canadians, relations with, in Upper Mississippi Valley, 31, 32.
Canoe, 125, 127; construction of leather, 13.
Carrollton, 130.
Carriage, 137.
Carry-all, 80, 118, 134.
Cart, 72, 131, 137.
Cartersville (Va.), 53, 57.
Causeway, 127.
Ce-se-ta, 81.
Chair, 136.
Chaise, 136.
Charleston (S. C.), 16, 27, 48; trading path leading from, 17; trade shifted from, 18, 20.
Chattahoochee River, 3, 4, 7, 16, 17, 48, 55, 81, 83, 104, 105, 119, 137.
Cherokee Indians, 6, 7, 24, 52, 61; population, 8; towns of, 16; trading path from Savannah to, 20; trading path from Augusta to, 20, 21; friendship and trade needed by English, 22; attitude toward trustees of Georgia, 23.
Chickasaw Agency, 63.
Chickasaw Bluffs, 8, 28, 65.
Chickasaw Indians, 7, 8, 17, 18, 24, 26, 27, 33, 34, 127; population, 8.
Choctaw Indians, 7, 8, 14, 24, 26, 27, 31, 35; population, 8; friendship and trade needed by English, 22,

23; treaty with, regarding opening of road, 35.
Christmas, Nathaniel, 56.
Chronicle (Augusta), 137.
Cincinnati, The, 107.
Claiborne (Ala.), mail route between, and Pensacola, 69.
Claiborne, William C. C., 35, 60, 90, 119.
Clarion (Nashville), 84.
Clarksborough (Ga.), 53, 54, 59.
Clifford, Joshua, letter to his daughter, Bess, 102, 103.
Coach, 131.
Colbert's Ferry, 128.
Collier, James, 64.
Colonies, Southern, 16; British, 38.
Columbia (S. C.), 78.
Columbus (Ga.), on the fall line, 3; tavern in, 104, 105, 119.
Commerce, Indian, 8, 9, 22; paths of, 12; in Pensacola, 32; in New Orleans, 35, 36; in Mobile, 84.
Conecah River, 86.
Conestoga wagon, 132, 133.
Conquistadore, influence on Indians, 15.
Constitutionalist (Augusta), 96.
Conveyance, Modes of, chapter VIII.
Coosa River, 7.
Corduroy road, 118, 129.
Cotton Port, 68.
"Covered wagon," 132.
Covington (Ga.), 106.
Creek Agency (Ga.), 87; distributing office for mail, 69.
Creek Indians, 6-8, 14, 15, 23-27, 84, 99, 106; population, 7; friendship and trade needed by English, 22.
Cumberland Valley, trading activity in, 28.
Cuming, Fortescue, 91.
Cuming, Sir Alexander, mission to the Cherokees, 16.

DAKIN and Dakin, 113.
Dale's Ferry, 128.
Danforth, James R., 109.

Danville (Va.), 57.
Darby, William, 91, 131.
Darien (Ga.), 442; communication between, and New Orleans, 41.
Dearborn, 80, 134.
Dearborn, Henry, 33.
De Leon, Ponce, 14.
De Luna, Tristán, 9, 14.
De Soto, Hernando, 9, 14, 95; boat constructed by, 11; landing, Tampa Bay, 14.
De Vaca, Alvar Nuñez Cabeça, 9, 14.
Deveaux, John, 122.
"Dug-out," 10.
Dutton, G., Lieutenant, 74.
Duty, on deer skins, 23.

EAGLE Tavern, 107.
Ebenezer, ferry at, 124.
Edinburgh Scotsman, 37.
Elizabeth City (N. C.), 94.
Elvas, Gentleman of, 11.
Emigration to the West, 137.
English, influence on Indians, 16, 22; traders, 17.
Escambia River, 86.
Essay on Plank Roads, William Gregg, 129.
Everitt, Josiah, 107.
Exchange Hotel, 110.

FALL line, effect on migration, 3, 95; proposed mail route following, 51.
Falls, of Savannah River, 21.
"Farmer's Railroad," 128.
Fayetteville (N. C.), 82.
Featherstonhough, G. W., 88, 104, 118.
Federal Road, 81.
Ferry, 14, 121, 122; treaty with Chickasaws regarding, 34; need of, 38, 43, 47, 87; location of, 42; to be established by surveyors, 44; over Tombigbee River, above St. Stephens, 54; over Alabama River, above Little River, 64; Mims, 68; at Line Creek, 83; improvement of, 117, 119 ff.; schedules of charges, 124 ff.
Filson, John, 32.
Finlay, Hugh, 126, 137.
Fisher, George, Colonel, 107.
Flats, 126.
Flint River, 4, 7, 16, 48, 54, 55.
Florence (Ala), 68.
Florida, 41; East and West, 27; inaccessibility of, by land, 38; road from Savannah to, 47.
"Forked country," 16, 48.
Fort Adams, 34, 35.
   Augusta (S. C.), 123.
   Bainbridge, 106.
   Barrington, ferry at, 124.
   Claiborne, road from Mobile to, 86.
   Gaines, 87.
   Hawkins, 65, 80, 87; road from, to St. Stephens, 66.
   Mitchell, 83, 87; post road from, to St. Stephens, 68; inn at, 89.
   Perry, 87.
   St. Stephens, 64; road from Fort Hawkins to, 66; post road from Fort Mitchell to, 68; distributing office for mail, 69.
   Stoddert, 53, 55, 94; road from Natchez to, 63; road from Fort Hawkins to, 65.
   Wilkinson, 128.
Franklin Court House (Ga.), 53, 58, 59.
Frederica (Ga.), 42.
Fredericksburg (Va.), 53, 57-59.
French, influence on Indians, 14-16, 22; church father, 14; trader, 14; in control of Louisiana, 30; philosophy of colonizing and trading, 30; Louisiana ceded by the, to United States, 35.
Frontier, trading, 16; Southern, safe from Indians and other enemies, 38; description of, conditions, 40, 41.
Fur trade, southern, 28, 36.

INDEX

GAINES Trace, 89.
Gallatin, Albert, communication from Thomas Jefferson to, 41; report of, submitted to the Senate, 64.
Gallier, J., 110.
Gazette of the State of Georgia, 127.
Gentleman's Magazine, 38.
Georgia, 4, 30, 42, 49, 65, 68, 72, 79, 82-84, 97, 104, 122, 130; termination of Alleghany Mountains in northern, 3, 51; Indian inhabitants of, 7; license to trade in, 19; difficulties between, and South Carolina, 23; emigrants moving from, 39, 81, 85, 90; emigrants in, 40, 41, 80, 88; surveyors in Province of, 43; organization of territory for road construction, 46; condition of travel in, 46 ff.; need of communication with New Orleans, 50; frontiers of, 55; road from, to New Orleans, 85, 86.
Gillespie, W. M., 128.
Gordon, Peter, 100.
Granger, Gideon, Postmaster General, 51.
Great Ogechee River, 122.
Gregg, William, 129.
Grubbs, John, 127.
Gulf of Mexico, 13.

HABERSHAM, James, 108.
Habersham, Joseph, 135.
Hamilton, John, Colonel, 94.
Hamilton, Thomas, 82.
Hampton, Wade, 119, 120.
Harris, Mrs., 106.
Hawkins, Benjamin, Colonel, 7, 34, 54, 59, 62, 90, 94.
Henry, Lemuel, 64.
Heustis, Jabez W., 93.
Hillsbrough, Earl of, 91.
Hodgson, Adam, 79-81.
Holt's Ferry, 128.
Hoss, Bishop, 99.
Hotel, City, 109.
  Exchange, 110.

State (Savannah), 108.
  Verandah, 113. *See* Appendix II.
"House for Strangers," 100.
Houses of entertainment, 85.
Huntsville (Ala.), 68, 114; distributing office for mail, 69, 70.
Hutchins, Thomas, 27, 92.

IMMIGRATION, 92; South of the Mountains, chapter III; into Louisiana, 93.
Indians, country inhabited by, 4, 33; coming of, 5; settling of, 6; war path for, 5; Creek, 6-8, 14, 15, 17, 22-24, 62, 84, 99; Cherokee, 6, 7, 16, 20, 22, 24, 52, 61, 62; Choctaw, 7, 8, 14, 22, 24, 31, 34, 35, 62; Chickasaw, 7, 8, 17, 18, 24, 33, 34, 127; Muskhogean, 7, 8; Creek population, 7; Seminole, 7; Chickasaw population, 8; Iroquoian, 8; Cherokee population, 8; Choctaw population, 8; commerce, 8, 9; trade, 9, 14, 16, 17, 20, 26, 27, 48; traces, 13; trading paths of, 9, 20, 33; trail, 3 ff.; bridge, 9, 88; in servitude, 12; attitude toward white man, 14, 23; French influence on, 14-16; Spanish influence on, 15, 16; English influence on, 16; regulation of trade, 19, 23, 24; traders, 19; objections of, to opening of roads, 33; treaty, 34; Southern Colonies as a barrier against, 38; Chickasaw Agency, 63; to maintain houses of entertainment, 63.
Indian towns, Upper Creek, 7; Lower Creek, 7; "over-the-hill," 8; Cese-ta, 81.
Inns, 63; Fort Mitchell, 89; and Taverns of the Old South, chapter VI. *See* Appendix II.
Iroquoian, 8.

JACKSON, Andrew, General, 67, 85.
Jackson, James, 51.
Jefferson, Thomas, communication

INDEX

from, to Albert Gallatin, 41; discussed plan for new mail route with Briggs, 52; commissioned Briggs to make preliminary survey, 53; communication from Briggs (Sept. 2, 1804), 53, 54; communication from Briggs (Oct. 1804), 54, 55; communication from Briggs (Nov. 26, 1804), 56, 57; submits reports of Briggs to Congress, 57; communication to Briggs (May 25, 1807), 60; communication from Lafayette to, 82.
Jersey wagon, 80, 133, 134.
Jesuits, 8.
Johnston, James W., Major, 89.
Jones, Noble Wimberley, 23.

K ATEEBEE Swamp, 119.
Kentucky, 37, 130; emigrants from, 90.
Ker, Henry, 121.
Killbeedy Creek, 118.
Knox, 7.
Knoxville (Tenn.), 51, 52, 65, 68, 78, 84; post route between and New Orleans, 61, 62; Creek road from, 63; stage line between, and Nashville, 68.
Kohl, J. G., 39.

L ACY, Roger, 21.
Lafayette, General, 81; letter from, to Jefferson, 82.
Lafitau, Jesuit Father, 8.
La Salle, 16.
Latrobe, Charles Joseph, 83.
Leigh, Walter, 120.
Lexington (Ky.), 72.
License, trading, 18, 24.
Line Creek, 83.
Little River, 64.
Loftus Heights, post road between, and New Orleans, 59.
Louisiana, 127, 130; French in control, 30; Indian trails in, 31; ceded to the United States, 35, 50; communication with, 41; interests in road building in, 59; problems in road building in, 60; emigration to, 92.
Lower Sauratown, 53.
Lower Trading Path, 48.

M ACKEY, Patrick, Captain, agent for Indian affairs in Georgia, 19.
McLean, Postmaster General, 70, 71, 78.
McMinn, Joseph, Governor, 68.
Macon (Ga.), on the fall line, 3.
Madison, James, 35.
Madisonville, 86.
Magruder, Allan B., 92.
Mail-coaches, 49, 88, 135.
Mail stage, 72.
Mail stage-coach, 135.
Manual of Road Making, W. M. Gillespie, 128.
Maps, lack of accurate, 39, 138.
Marathon, 68.
Martin, Francois Xavier, 94.
Martyn, Benjamin, 122.
Meigs, R. J., communication from, to Charles Bell, 67.
Melish, John, 79.
Memphis (Tenn.), 8.
Meriwether, General, 54.
Middlesex Ferry, 126.
Middle Trading Path, 48, 79, 84.
Military Road, 85.
Milledgeville (Ga.), 80, 84, 94; road from, to New Orleans, 41.
Mill-Town, two ferries at, 124.
Mims Ferry, 68.
Mingo, 34.
Mississippi, 37, 50, 65, 91, 97; fall line in the state of, 3; Chickasaw territory, 8; Choctaw territory, 8; emigrants in, 41, 80; problems in road building in southern, 60.
Mississippi River, 22, 24, 30, 34, 49, 63, 79, 82, 84, 85, 90-92, 94; English traders reach, 17.
Mississippi Territory, 52.
Mississippi Valley, French and Spanish influence in, 16; trade in, 30;

relations with Canadians in, 31, 32; need of communication between, and Washington, 50.
Mitchell, General, 87.
Mitchell, Samuel L., 50.
Mobile (Ala.), 25, 56, 65, 78, 80, 82, 91, 101; traffic between, and Montgomery, 4; French influence at, 22; as trading center, 26, 27, 29, 30, 84; loyal Britons residing in, 28; exports from (1823-24), 29; path from the Ocmulgee to, 62; road from Augusta to, 81, 82; road from, to Fort Claiborne, 86; road from Pensacola to, 89; road from Natchez, 128.
Mobile Bay, 4, 26, 84, 86.
Monette, John W., 64.
Monroe, James, 41.
Montgomery (Ala.), 3, 78, 82, 130; traffic between, and Mobile, 4; first stage route east from, 89.
Moore, Francis, 11.
"Mud-roads," 130.
Muscle Shoals, of the Tennessee River, 3.
Muskhogean, 7, 8.
Mutteer's Landing, 125.

NARVAEZ, 9.
Nashville (Tenn.), 28, 51, 64; road from, to Natchez, 66; stage line between Knoxville and, 68; road from, to New Orleans, 85.
Natchez (Miss.), 33, 51, 53, 64, 68, 72, 78, 87, 91, 94, 101, 132; road from, to Fort Stoddert, 63; road from Nashville to, 66; distributing office for mail, 70; relinquished by Spanish, 90; road from Mobile, 128.
Natchez Trace, 89, 91.
National Road, 72.
National Road from Washington to New Orleans, letter from Calhoun to governor of Georgia concerning, 73; board of engineers for, 74; three routes of, 74; characteristics of routes compared, 74, 75; value of each route to commerce, 75, to population, 75, to defense, 75, to mail, 76; specifications for, 76; estimate of cost of, 76; need for preservation of, 77.
New France, expansion of, 16.
New Orleans (La.), 27, 28, 50, 55, 56, 60, 65, 67, 80, 82, 87, 93-95, 101, 132; as trading center, 30, 32, 92; Indian trails converging at, 31; future of, assured, 35; importance of communication with, 41; road between Milledgeville and, 41; road from Savannah to, 47; route between, and Washington, 51, 52, 61, 72, 74, 78; post road between Loftus Heights and, 59, 60; post route between Knoxville and, 61; Battle of, 66, 67; road from Georgia to, 85, 86; road from Nashville to, 85; stage between Baton Rouge and, 91; taverns in, 109 ff.; road from, to Carrollton, 130.
New York (N. Y.), 66.
Nicholson, Governor of Maryland, 16.
Nicolls, Colonel, 62.
Niles' Weekly Register, 67, 74.
Norfolk (Va.), 82.
North Carolina, 84; emigrants move from, 39, 90; emigrants in, 40.

OCAIN, Daniel, 108.
Ocmulgee River, 3, 4, 17, 62.
Oconee River, 4, 17, 128.
Oglethorpe, James, 16, 19, 20, 22, 23, 42, 121.
Ohio River, 72, 82, 92.
Ordinaries, 99.
Ottolenghe, Joseph, 23.
Outlaws of Cave-in Rock, by Otto Rothert, 65.
"Over-the-hill" settlements, 8, 16, 24.

PANTON, Leslie and Company, 28; stores at St. Mark's, Pensacola, and Mobile, 28.

Parish of St. Paul, 123.
Park, James, 68.
Park, William, 68.
Pascagoula River, 56.
Paths, determining factors for location of, 6; Upper Trading, 8, 48; trading, of Indians, 9; of commerce, 12; trading, 14, 16 ff.; converging at Augusta, 21; between Savannah and Augusta, 21, 48; improvement of, 33, 35; Middle Trading Path, 48, 79; Lower Trading Path, 48.
Pearl River, 4, 53, 56, 63, 64.
Pensacola (Fla.), 25-27, 81; loyal Britons residing in, 28; commerce in, 32; Virginians in, 38; mail route between Claiborne and, 69; road from, to Mobile, 89.
Philadelphia (Pa.), 66.
Pickens, Andrew, 34.
Pickett, Albert James, Colonel, 89.
Piedmont line of stages, 84.
Pine Bluff, 122, 124-26.
Piragua, 10; method of construction, 10, 11.
Plank road, 128.
Point Comfort, 56, 57, 59, 81.
Pontchartrain, Lake, 24, 86.
Pope, John, 92, 120.
Population, Creek, 7; Chickasaw, 8; Cherokee, 8; Choctaw, 8.
Portmanteau, 70.
Postal service, 50; distribution offices in Old Southwest, 69, 70; cost of handling mail, 70; methods of handling mail recommended by the Department, 71, 72.
Post roads, development of, chapter IV; between Loftus Heights and New Orleans, 59; between Knoxville and New Orleans, 61; between Fort Mitchell and St. Stephens, 68; between Claiborne and Pensacola, 69; between Washington and New Orleans, 78; through the southern capitals to Mobile, 78; by way of Augusta, Ga., Montgomery, and Mobile, 78.

Poussin, W. T., Captain, 74.
Pritchard, B. O., 113.
Public-houses, 99.

R ABUN, William, Governor, 87.
"Raccoon bridge," 117.
Raft, method of construction, 11.
Raleigh (N. C.), 82.
Randolph, John, 37.
Ranjel, 11; describes method of crossing stream, 12.
Revolutionary War, paths during, 21; English influence on Indians during, 25; organization of territory inhabited by Indians after, 32.
Rivers—
  Alabama, 3, 4, 7, 17, 26, 28, 56, 59, 64, 84, 86, 89, 128.
  Altamaha, 4, 42, 46, 121, 125.
  Apalachicola, 4.
  Cahawba, 80.
  Chattahoochee, 3, 4, 7, 16, 17, 48, 55, 81, 83, 104, 105, 119, 137.
  Conecah, 86.
  Coosa, 7.
  Escambia, 86.
  Flint, 4, 7, 16, 48, 54, 55.
  Great Ogechee, 47, 122.
  Little, 64.
  Mississippi, 22, 24, 30, 34, 49, 63, 79, 82, 84, 85, 90-92, 94.
  Oconee, 4, 17, 128.
  Ocmulgee, 3, 4, 17, 62.
  Ohio, 72, 82, 92.
  Pascagoula, 56.
  Pearl, 4, 53, 56, 63, 64.
  Savannah, 3, 4, 21, 48, 119, 120.
  Sip-se, 13.
  St. Mary's, 46.
  Tallapoosa, 7, 56, 57, 59.
  Tennessee, 3.
  Tensaw, 86.
  Tombigbee, 4, 26, 28, 52, 56, 57, 84, 89.
Road, buffalo, 5; objections of Indians to the opening of, 33; treaty with Chickasaws regarding, 34; treaty

190　INDEX

with Choctaws regarding, 34, 35; need of, 38, 87; emigration along, 41; between Milledgeville and New Orleans, 41; authorized by Colonial Assembly (1735), 41, 42; condition of early, 42, 47; duties of surveyors of, 43; specification for the, 44; schedule of fines, 45; organization of territory for, construction, 46; Southwest, 46; radiating from Savannah, 47; from Augusta to Savannah, 48, 49; repair of, 59; problems in, building in Louisiana and southern Mississippi, 60; from Tellico to Tombigbee River, 62; from Natchez to Fort Stoddert, 63; Creek, from Knoxville, 63; "three-chopped way," 64; from Nashville to Natchez, 66; from Fort Hawkins to St. Stephens, 66; National Road from Washington to New Orleans, 72; Federal Road, 81; condition of (1806-1830), 79 ff.; from Augusta to Mobile, 81, 82; Military Road, 85; Gaines Trace, 89; Bolivar Indian Trail, 89; Natchez Trace, 89, 91; Robinson Road, 89; from Mobile to Pensacola, 89; improvement of, chapter VII; corduroy, 118, 129; from Mobile to Natchez, 128; Plank road, 128; "Farmer's Railroad," 128; Shell road, 130; turnpike-roads, 130; "mud-roads," 130.
Robertson, Thomas, assistant to Isaac Briggs, 54.
Robinson Road, 89.
Rochester (S. C.), 123.
Rothert, Otto, 65.
Rowell, Edward, 120.
Rowland, Mrs. Dunbar, 97.

St. Augustine (Fla.), 20, 25; loyal Britons residing in, 28.
St. Genevieve, road from, to Chickasaw Bluffs, 65.
St. Louis Day, 56.
St. Mark's, 28.
St. Mary's River, 46.
St. Stephens, 86.
Salisbury (N. C.), 53, 57-59.
Salt licks, sought by wild animals, 4.
Santa Sevilia, 125.
Savannah (Ga.), 27, 42, 47, 65, 96, 107, 108, 121; travel from, to Augusta, Ga., 4; founded 1733, 16, 18, 41; as trading center, 18, 20, 26; trading needs of, 19; paths radiating from, 20; travel down Savannah River to, 21; extent of trade at (1749-1821), 25; path from Barnwell's Bluff to, 42; public wharf at, 46; need of road from, to Great Ogeechee, 47; road from, to Augusta, 47-49, 80; road from, to Florida, 47; road from, to New Orleans, 47; distributing office for mail, 69; first tavern in, 100.
Savannah Coffee House, 108.
Savannah River, 3, 4, 21, 48, 119, 120; falls of, 21; ferry across, 123, 124, 126, 127.
Seminole Indians, 7.
Semple, Ellen Churchill, 3.
Shell road, 130.
Short, John, 72.
Shriver, David, 74.
Sip-se River, 13.
Skows, 126.
Slaves, transported in the South, 80, 81.
Smyth, J. F. D., 114.
Somerville, 68.
South Carolina, 68, 82; Indian trade, 17; difficulties between Georgia and, 23; emigrants move from, 39, 81, 85, 90; emigrants in, 40.
Southwest, Old, 3, 4, 138.
Spanish, bridge, 10; influence on Indians, 15, 16, 22; influence in New Orleans, 35; Natchez relinquished by, 90.
Stage-coach, 47, 70, 71, 83, 134.
State Hotel, 107.
Stebbins, Burt and, 109.
Stirling, James, 130.
Stork, William, 38.

INDEX   191

Stuart, John, 23; plan of reorganization of Indian trade, 23, 24.
Sulkies, covered, 71.
Superintendent of Indian affairs, 23; John Stuart, 23; Edmond Atkins, 23.
Surveyors, appointed in Province of Georgia (1755), 43; duties of, 43, 44; schedule of fines, 45; organization of territory for road construction, 46.
Sutcliffe, Robert, 137.

TALLAPOOSA River, 7, 56, 57, 59.
Tampa Bay, 14.
Tavern, 63; Inns and, of the Old South, chapter VI; Tondee's, 107; Eagle, 107. See Hotels, Inns, Appendix II.
Taylor, Wm., 69.
Tellico Block House, 52, 61, 62.
Tennessee, 94, 130; emigrants from, 90.
Tennessee River, 3.
Tensaw River, 86.
Texas, 65.
Thomas, David, 51, 52.
Thompson, William, 108.
"Three-chopped way," 64.
"Three Sisters" Ferry, 126.
Toll bridge, 119; Augusta, 119 ff., schedule of charges (1791), 120, "Yazoo freshet" (1796), 120, schedule of charges (1809), 120.
Tombigbee River, 4, 26, 28, 52, 56, 57, 84, 89; road from Tellico to, 62; ferry on, above Fort St. Stephens, 64.
Tondee's Tavern, 107.
Toulmir, Harry, 64.
Towns, Upper Creek, 7; Lower Creek, 7, 17; "over-the-hill," 8.
Traces, Indian, 3 ff.
Trade, objects of Indian, 8, 19, 20; barter, 8; Indian, 9, 14, 16, 17, 27, 28, in South Carolina, 17; Savannah as center of, 18, 25; with Chickasaw Indians, 18; illegal, 19; regulation of, 19, 23, 24; warranting improvement of trails, 21; with Cherokees, Creeks, Choctaws, 22; extent of trade at Savannah (1749-1821), 25; Mobile as center of, 26, 29, 30; fur, in South, 28; price list (1716) published in Paris, 30, 31; price list (1729), 32; American, in Louisiana, 35.
Trader, early, 3, 13; French, 14; English, 17, 21, 22; Indian, 17, 19; description of, in Georgia, 18; of Carolina, 23; paths used by, 47.
Trading license, 18-20; renewal of, 18; method of issuing, 24.
Trading paths, of early settlers, 16 ff.; location of, 17; condition of, 17; radiating from Savannah, 20; Savannah to St. Augustine, 20; Savannah to Augusta, 20; from Augusta, 20.
Trading-posts, 13, 16.
Trails, Indian, 3 ff.; animal, 5, 6; converging at Augusta, 21; between Savannah and Augusta, 21; converging at New Orleans, 31.
Transportation, river, handicapped by fall line, 3; as related to Indian trade, 17; cheap, needed, 28; improvements in, chapter VII.
Transshipment, three types of, 21; Augusta, a point of, 21; Savannah, a point of, 21; Mobile, a point of, 26.
Transylvania University, 65.
Travel, early, 13; difficulty of, 47; rate of, in transporting mail, 65, 66.
Traveler, early, 3; on the road, chapter V.
Treaty, with the Chickasaws, 34; with the Choctaws, 34.
Trimble T., Lieutenant, 74.
Tuckanbatchee, 53.
Turnpike-roads, 130.

UNION Society, 107.
University of Georgia, 104.
Upper Trading Path, 8.

VEHICLES—
  Carriage, 137.
  Carry-all, 80.
  Cart, 72, 131, 137.
  Chair, 136.
  Chaise, 136.
  Coach, 131.
  Conestoga wagon, 132, 133.
  Covered sulkies, 71.
  "Covered wagon," 132.
  Dearborn, 80.
  Jersey wagon, 80, 133, 134.
  Mail-coach, 49, 88, 135.
  Mail stage, 72.
  Mail stage-coach, 134.
  Stage-coach, 47, 70, 71, 83, 134.
  Wagon, 47, 80, 131, 137.
Verandah, The (hotel), 113.
Virginia, emigrants move from, 39, 90.
Volney, C. F., 12.

WAGON, 47, 80, 131, 137.
Walton, Judge, 49, 79.
War of 1812, 66.
Washington (D. C.), 51, 58, 59; need of communication between, and New Orleans, 50; route between, and New Orleans, 51, 61, 72, 78.
Washington, George, in Georgia (1791), 49, 120.
Way-bag, 70.
Western Gazetteer, 86.
West Florida, 91.
Westward movement, paths of, 3 ff.
Whitaker, Arthur Preston, 28.
Whitefield, George, Reverend, 42.
Wilkins, Jane, 72.
Wright, Joseph, 123.

"YAZOO Freshet," 120.

"ZUBLY'S" Ferry, 127.

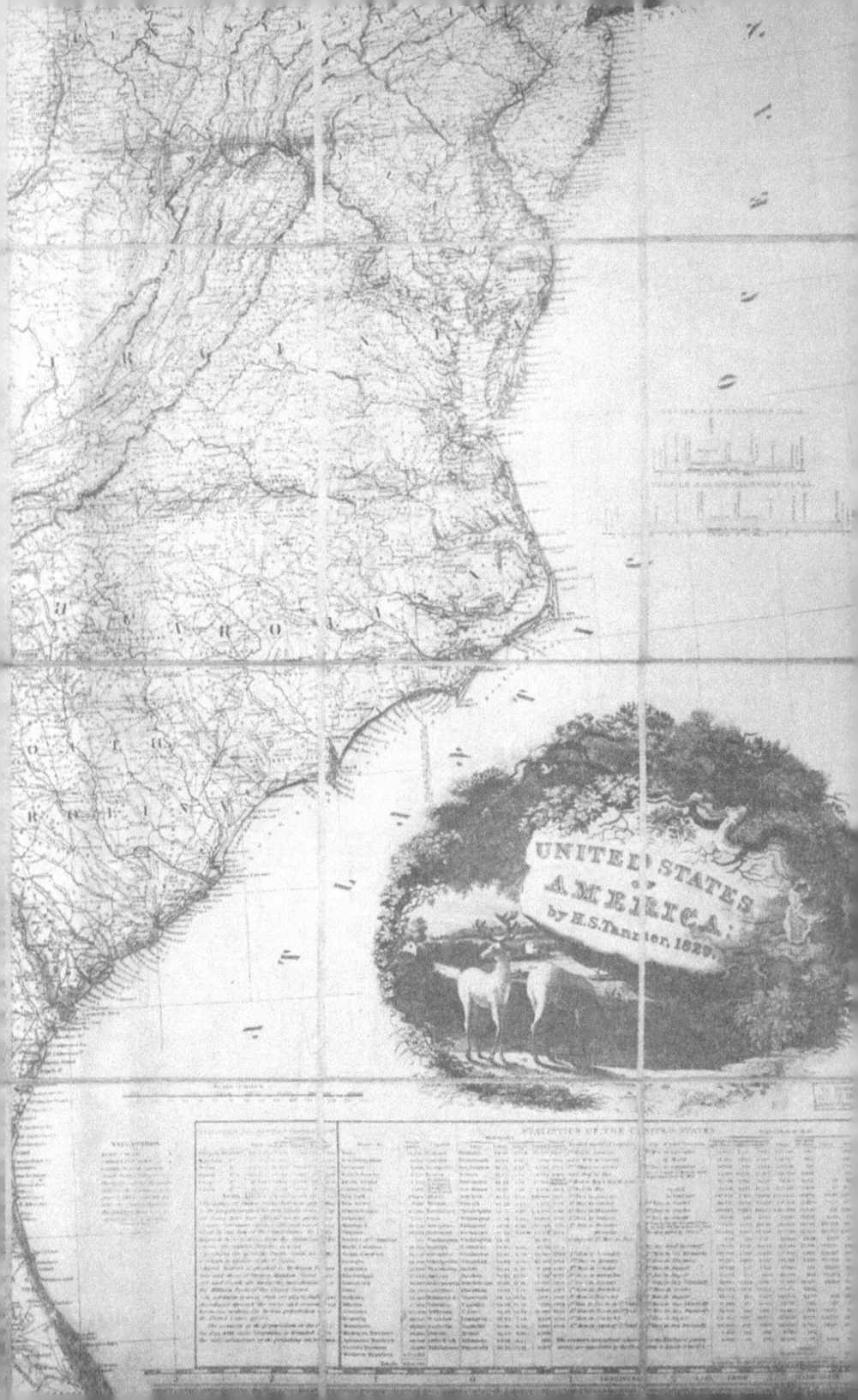

www.ingramcontent.com/pod-product-compliance
Lightning Source LLC
Chambersburg PA
CBHW021404290426
44108CB00010B/377